"Mindfulness for Teens with ADHD nails it! Any teen—indeed, any *person*—who has ADHD can gain enormously by using this practical, reader-friendly, immensely valuable workbook. The author knows her stuff, having worked in the real world of teens and attention deficit/ hyperactivity disorder (ADHD) for years. I give this book the highest recommendation. It will reduce stress, build skills, and dramatically improve the life of every person who uses it."

—**Edward Hallowell, MD**, coauthor of *Driven to Distraction*

"Mindfulness at its core is about building attention, increasing self-awareness, and creating new choices in responding. This makes a mindfulness-based approach a perfect fit for those who have unique brain functioning and learning styles such as in ADHD. Debra Burdick's invaluable book provides teens, and those that work with them, with an excellent blueprint for applying curiosity and kindness to one's ADHD characteristics, weaknesses, and strengths. The book goes to the heart of typical teen struggles such as schoolwork or making friends, and through structured questions and practices guides the teen reader to simultaneously become more self-accepting and more resourceful in dealing with daily challenges."

—**Lidia Zylowska, MD**, associate professor in the department of psychiatry at University of Minnesota, founding member at UCLA Mindful Awareness Research Center, and author of *The Mindfulness Prescription for Adult ADHD*

"Debra Burdick has done it again! Another step-by-step, easy-to-follow book—and this time, for teens with ADHD. Burdick takes us from home and school all the way to employment and long-term success with her mindfulness activities. This book is a must for all those working with teens, and also for all teens, whether they have ADHD or not."

—**Susan Epstein, LCSW**, parenting expert and business coach for therapists, coaches, and healers; author of *Over 60 Techniques, Activities, and Worksheets for Challenging Children and Adolescents*

"I've seen first-hand how mindfulness can help people with ADHD. In her new book, *Mindfulness for Teens with ADHD*, Debra Burdick gives you some powerful techniques to help teens with ADHD succeed in all areas of their lives. The book is full of practical tools that teens can use in a variety of situations. I highly recommend it."

—**Charles A. Francis**, author of *Mindfulness Meditation Made Simple*

"In my practice in sleep medicine and child neurology, I've seen first-hand the power that cultivating mindfulness can have. This is an excellent resource for learning mindfulness, which is divided up nicely into segments that a teen with ADHD can easily follow to help them in all areas of their life."

—**Jose Colon, MD, MPH**, founder of Paradise Sleep, and award-winning author of books on sleep for women, children, and infants

"As a former high school teacher, I have seen many methods to support teenagers with ADHD, and at the core of all successful techniques is *mindfulness*. Debra Burdick has compiled an amazing toolkit for parents and teachers to use with their teens to help them focus, become more aware, and ultimately increase their self-confidence. These activities will be a part of their lifetime daily care habits, and good for everyone to use."

—**Julie Kleinhans**, youth empowerment and education mentor, and creator of Successful Kids Revolution and Mind Focus Generation

"*Mindfulness for Teens with ADHD* is a fabulous tool for both parents and teens. Debra has organized a step-by-step process which takes the overwhelm out of living with ADHD. This book is a must-have for all teens."

—**Heather Chauvin**, founder of Mom Is In Control

mindfulness for teens with adhd

a skill-building workbook to help you focus & succeed

DEBRA BURDICK, LCSW

Instant Help Books
An Imprint of New Harbinger Publications, Inc.

Publisher's Note

Distributed in Canada by Raincoast Books

Copyright © 2017 by Debra Burdick
        Instant Help Books
        An Imprint of New Harbinger Publications, Inc.
        5674 Shattuck Avenue
        Oakland, CA 94609
        www.newharbinger.com

Cover design by Amy Shoup

Acquired by Wendy Millstine

Edited by Karen Schaeder

Library of Congress Cataloging-in-Publication Data on file

Printed in the United States of America

19   18   17

10   9   8   7   6   5   4   3   2   1   First printing

I gratefully dedicate this book to my love and husband,
Al Zipperle, who showed me that being present and enjoying
the moments gives you a life full of good moments.
Thank you, Al. I love you.

Contents

Section 4: How to Live a Healthy Life

Section 5: Creating Success

Foreword

If ADHD is occasional or frequent mindlessness, mindfulness is part of the solution. Debra Burdick's book is immediately useful for creating positive steps forward. For parents, it is time we tell our teens a different story. Instead of telling them they have broken brains as a way of understanding ADHD, let's tell them that the harder they work to train their attention, the more they can be the bosses of their brains.

No longer will we tell teens that their brains are broken so they think, *Why try?* and lose their motivation. When they stop trying, they begin to fail, and they lose self-esteem and the opportunity to grow their brains. Imagine the difference between telling a teen that he has a brain disorder and telling him that he can be a brain athlete and rewire his own brain if he works hard enough. A different story means a different outcome.

It is important to remember that if mindfulness is nonjudgmental awareness, in contrast the diagnosis of ADHD comes with clear judgments in the very words "deficit" and "disorder." It can help to see your very symptoms through the lens of nonjudgment. What are you doing when you are not paying attention? Is it possible that what distracts you is also what interests you, so you learn more about who you are in observing your distractibility without judging it?

Debra's book starts with the basics and adds simple steps to create change. Early on, she introduces the foundational skill of setting intentions. You may start with an intention to get good grades or to get more sleep. She helps you dig deep to find the motivation by asking yourself a few questions: "Why do I want to do this?" "What will I accomplish?" "What is the purpose of this intention?"

This book is designed for the teen with a short attention span. For the teens who are reading this, you can dip in for a few minutes and get a few reminders that immediately set your track in a new direction. Debra will show you how to use mindfulness to prepare for exams and to manage emotional roller coasters. The good news here is that the latest research shows us that we can change our brains through neuroplasticity. The more you practice, the easier it gets to stay focused and pay attention. Mindfulness will help treat ADHD, and it will also do more: it will create a tool for emotional regulation and self-control that will last your whole life.

You will find specific tips on how to get to sleep, how to stay focused while driving, and how to manage your diet. One obvious benefit of this mindfulness approach is that there are no negative side effects. Some find that with medications they habituate over time, and old problems return. You may find you need higher doses. With mindfulness, the longer you practice these tools, the more potent their impact becomes on your life. This book is a fundamental tool in your ADHD toolbox.

No one doubts that teens today are challenged with an epidemic of stress and often unmanageable demands. These challenges are magnified for teens with ADHD. I often tell my clients, "The fastest way to change your state is to change your breathing." This book offers dozens of tools and reminders of this simplest, most effective tool for stress management. Stress-management skills are a requirement for any teen with ADHD, and this book offers quick tips and quick fixes.

—Dr. Lara Honos-Webb, author of *The Gift of ADHD*, *The ADHD Workbook for Teens*, http://www.addisagift.com

A Letter to Teens with ADHD

Hey! What's up? Welcome! I am delighted that you and this book found each other.

As a teen with ADHD, you face all the typical demands that most teens face. But you probably already know that having ADHD can make it much harder to successfully meet all those demands. You may feel like you have to work twice as hard as everyone else. You may feel frustrated, stressed out, exhausted, and maybe even like giving up sometimes.

This workbook will give you a set of skills you can use to thrive and succeed in spite of, and maybe even because of, your ADHD. You will learn mindfulness skills that will help you succeed in all areas of your life.

I encourage you to skim through the workbook to get a sense of how it might help you with specific challenges you are dealing with right now. As you do that, mark the activities you think will help you the most, and then number them in order of importance to you. This will help you stay on track and get the benefits more quickly.

Section 1 will help you understand and embrace your ADHD and be mindful of how it shows up in your life. If you need help improving your ability to organize and concentrate and do better in school, pay particular attention to the activities for mindfulness at home and school in section 2. To get along better with others (even your parents) and feel better about yourself, focus on the activities in section 3. If you don't get enough sleep and feel tired all the time, or you don't eat well, or you are wondering about the impact of drugs or alcohol on your life, or if you are driving, look carefully at the activities in Section 4. And if you want to get a part-time job or plan your future, the activities for creating success in section 5 will be especially valuable.

After you have skimmed through the book, go back and start at the beginning. Although you may be tempted to skip over the first section, please focus on its four activities and complete them before going on. They provide a foundation for the rest of the activities. Then do the remaining activities in order, or if you feel it works better for you, do the activities in the order that you marked earlier to help you with the things you struggle with the most or need help with right now.

Practicing mindfulness skills can help you rewire your brain in areas that help you concentrate, motivate yourself, organize, and feel better. Although you may be skeptical at first, chances are good that you will benefit in all these areas. Keep in mind that you will get the most benefit from the book if you work through the whole book and complete each activity. Be prepared to spend some time doing this. Don't worry if it takes you a few months. Perhaps you can plan to complete at least one or two activities per week. You can set a reminder on your calendar app for when to do the activities each week.

As you complete each activity and learn and practice the skills, you will notice that you can apply them to many different situations in your life. And you will discover that you can use them for the rest of your life!

Some of the activities involve guided imagery scripts for going within and using the power of your mind and imagination to create success in your life. You will find audio recordings of these online at http://www.newharbinger.com/36255. As you do these activities, follow the instructions at the back of the book to download the accompanying audios to your phone, tablet, or computer so you can listen to them periodically throughout your day. Some activities include forms you can download and print, again following the instructions at the back of the book.

Some teens with ADHD worry that they can't focus their attention within themselves and calm their minds and bodies. If this is you, don't worry. Most of the mindfulness guided-imagery skills in this book are very brief, and you will find the process gets easier and easier with practice. Much like learning to ride a bike—it may seem hard and uncomfortable at first, but it will get easier with practice as your brain learns how to do it, until it eventually becomes automatic. Start with brief times and increase gradually.

The more you focus on completing the activities, the more you can change your brain and your life for the better and truly thrive with ADHD.

Turn to section 1, and let's get going!

A Letter to Parents of Teens with ADHD

As the mother of an adult daughter with ADHD, I know how challenging and at the same time absolutely wonderful and rewarding parenting teens with ADHD can be. These teens must deal with the normal demands that all teens have to face, but symptoms of ADHD often make this dramatically more difficult. They frequently feel frustrated, angry, irritable, anxious, and afraid they are failures. On the other hand, their enthusiasm, energy, intelligence, creativity, sharp wit, and ability to think outside the box are gifts that can help them truly thrive.

Take time to learn everything you possibly can about ADHD and what you can do to help your son or daughter succeed. As you parent, ask yourself, *What does my teen need from me right now?* Keep in mind that teens always need their parents' unconditional love, understanding, encouragement, guidance, and support. Be aware of what they are learning from you as a role model.

Think about how ADHD impacts the relationship you have, as well as your expectations and your ability to trust them with appropriate responsibilities and independence. If they inherited their ADHD from you, be mindful of how your own ADHD impacts your ability to be organized and consistent as parents.

This workbook is designed to help teens become more mindful of how ADHD shows up in their lives and to learn specific mindfulness skills that will help them navigate the normal everyday tasks they must complete in order to succeed at home, in school, in their relationships, in living a healthy life, and in work and beyond.

Although the workbook is written directly to teens, you can help them use it and encourage them to stay on track if they have difficulty doing so on their own. Depending on their independence and skill levels, you may review each activity with them, support them in completing the activities, ask them how or when they will do an activity, and remind them to schedule it on their calendar app. An incentive to help them motivate themselves to do each activity can be useful, such as spending time with a friend when they complete one. Review the benefits of each activity with them, and support them in reflecting on how doing an activity has helped them.

They will benefit from doing all forty activities, but encourage them to complete the first four and to then do the rest in the order that best meets their specific needs. For example, if their bedroom is in chaos or they are having trouble organizing their homework, suggest that they do the "Organizing Your Space" or "Organizing Your Schoolwork" activities first. Or if they put themselves down a lot or feel stressed out, they could do the "Taming Your Inner Critic" or "De-stressing Instantly" activities first. Numbering the activities in order of personal importance can help them stay on track and get the benefits more quickly.

Some of the activities have recorded meditations that are available to download at http://www .newharbinger.com/36255. Following the instructions at the back of the book, help them access and download these, and make sure they have a quiet place they can listen to them where they won't be disturbed. Other activities have forms that can be downloaded via the same link, and printed.

Take time to be present as a parent. Listen to your teens. Show them you understand them. Show them your love. I encourage you to truly enjoy each moment with your teens. You will have a deeper connection with them, and you will both have a more meaningful journey.

A Letter to Professionals

Whether you are a mental health professional, an educator, a coach, or anyone who helps teens with ADHD, you have a remarkable opportunity to help them embrace their unique gifts and abilities while guiding them and teaching them skills that help them thrive.

This workbook is written directly to teens with ADHD and provides them with mindfulness skills to help them succeed in every area of their lives. As a helper, you are in an excellent position to assist teens so that they get the most benefit from this workbook.

Here's a step-by-step process for helping teens work through the activities in this book:

1. Do activities 1–4. These activities provide a basis for doing the rest of them, so be sure teens do these four first.

2. After they've done activities 1–4, skim through the table of contents with the teens and have them place checkmarks beside the activities they need the most help with. Then ask them to number those they checked off in order of importance to them. If the activities all look equally important, then they can do them in the order in the book.

3. Do the rest of the activities either in order or according to how they numbered them in step 2.

4. For each activity:

   * Read through it together. Discuss what they need to do, when and where they will do it, and how much time they need to allow for it.

   * Complete the activity together, or if they are not doing it with you, encourage them to schedule a time to do it on their calendar app.

5. After they've done each activity, follow these steps:

   * Discuss their answers to the questions asked in the activity.

   * Explore how they implemented the skill.

   * Explore what they learned about themselves from the activity.

   * Discuss what challenges they had doing it and how they did or could handle them.

   * Help them reflect on how they felt doing the activity.

   * Ask how the skill helped them or may help them in the future.

   * Discuss how and when they will continue to implement the skill they learned.

6. Help them stay on track.

   * Plan which activities to do next.

   * Find a time to do each activity, and encourage them to put it in their calendar app with a reminder alert.

   * If they didn't do the activity as planned, explore why and what they need to do next time to make sure they do it.

   * Discuss and handle their objections to doing the activities. (Examples: no time, forgot, don't see why it would help, got distracted, too hard, felt overwhelmed)

   * Remind them of the benefits, and explore how they think their life might be better if a particular activity helped them.

   * Explore how they motivate themselves (usually to avoid pain or gain pleasure) and what they can do to motivate themselves to do the work involved in learning and practicing the skills in this book.

Be patient as you help teens work through these activities. Remember that having ADHD means they struggle with executive functions, such as planning, organizing, paying attention, completing tasks, impulse control, emotional regulation, self-monitoring, and initiating activity. These are exactly the areas the skills in this workbook will improve, but most teens with ADHD become easily distracted and intensely frustrated, so they will need your help to stay motivated and on task to complete the activities.

Think about what they need most from you, such as acceptance, guidance, encouragement, and reminders. Help them create systems for staying on track to complete all the activities they deem most helpful. Show them your positive expectation that they can master all the skills in this workbook as long as they don't give up.

Thank you for helping teens embrace these mindfulness skills, skills that will significantly change their lives.

Section 1

Being Mindful About Your ADHD

ADHD can impact your life in many ways. The first step in making beneficial changes in your life is to stop and become mindful of both the helpful and unhelpful ways that ADHD affects you. When you accept and understand your ADHD symptoms, you can learn specific skills to help you thrive.

This section explains what mindfulness is and why being mindful is important for those with ADHD. The activities can help you become more aware of the challenges as well as the joys of having ADHD, and guide you in finding the support you need. They also teach you a process for setting your intention to help you stay on track and achieve your goals.

1 what is mindfulness and why should you care?

for you to know

Mindfulness is paying attention to something that you choose or need to pay attention to. Teens with ADHD often have trouble paying attention. Learning and practicing mindfulness skills can help you improve your concentration and be more successful in everything you do. You can be mindful any time, such as when you are walking, having a conversation, doing your homework, or even learning to drive.

Alice often had trouble paying attention and didn't get her schoolwork or homework done on time. She felt embarrassed and frustrated when she received a failing grade because she got distracted and didn't finish a test. When she learned that mindfulness involved paying attention to something in particular, she realized that when she got distracted she forgot to pay attention to the test she was taking.

During her next test, she set her intention to pay attention to the test, and as soon as she noticed she was distracted, she brought her attention back to the test—over and over again. It was a lot of work to keep bringing her attention back, but it got easier with practice. She learned not to beat herself up for getting distracted. And she noticed that she loved how she felt when she finished a test on time and got a good grade.

She learned that she could be mindful at any time. She practiced being mindful of her surroundings, thoughts, feelings, behavior, and choices.

for you to do

Renowned psychologist Jon Kabat-Zinn, who specializes in mindfulness-based stress reduction, has defined mindfulness as "paying attention in a particular way: on purpose, in the present moment, and nonjudgmentally." Mindfulness coach Amy Saltzman has defined it as "paying attention to your life, here and now, with kindness and curiosity," and mindfulness teacher Susan Kaiser-Greenland as "being aware of what is happening as it's happening." My own definition is "paying attention to what's going on right here, right now, inside of us or outside of us."

Circle the definition you like best, and then write down what all four have in common.

_____

_____

_____

Write your own definition here:

_____

_____

_____

Do you have trouble paying attention? Write down three activities during which you get distracted. (Examples: homework, chores, tests, getting ready in the morning)

1. _____

2. _____

3. _____

Write down three times you were mindful this week:

1. _____

2. _____

3. _____

... and more to do

Write down the three most important things to be mindful of (to pay attention to) while:

- getting ready in the morning

  a. _____

  b. _____

  c. _____

- sitting in the classroom

  a. _____

  b. _____

  c. _____

- talking to a classmate

  a. _____

  b. _____

  c. _____

- hanging out with friends

  a. _____

  b. _____

  c. _____

- talking to your parents

  a. _____

  b. _____

  c. _____

- doing homework

  a. _____

  b. _____

  c. _____

- doing your chores

  a. _____

  b. _____

  c. _____

- getting to bed on time

  a. _____

  b. _____

  c. _____

- making good choices about drugs and alcohol

  a. _____

  b. _____

  c. _____

- organizing your stuff

  a. _____

  b. _____

  c. _____

- deciding where to go to college

  a. _____

  b. _____

  c. _____

- driving

  a. _____

  b. _____

  c. _____

2 being mindful of how ADHD shows up in your life

for you to know

The first step in improving your ability to thrive as a teen with ADHD is to become aware (mindful) of how ADHD shows up in your life, both in good and bad ways. When you understand how ADHD impacts your life, you will be better prepared to do what you need to do to minimize any unhelpful impact and maximize helpful impact.

Alyssa felt very frustrated and wished she didn't have ADHD. She wrote down all the ways ADHD got in her way and made her life harder. She hated how hard it was to stay organized. She wished she had more friends and worried that her hyperactivity and impulsivity might be in the way of her learning how to get along better with people. As she did this exercise, she became more mindful of her symptoms and started to notice how much her ADHD symptoms impacted her life.

Then she wrote down what she liked about having ADHD and discovered there were some things she really enjoyed about it. She liked being creative and able to think outside the box. She loved her energy and enthusiasm for doing things. She realized that her life was often really fun.

for you to do

Take some time to think about how ADHD impacts your life, and then fill in the lines below with a few words to indicate the many ways it does. Be specific. Include both helpful and unhelpful ways. Use an extra sheet of paper if needed.

ADHD is helpful to me in these ways:

_____

_____

_____

_____

_____

_____

_____

ADHD is unhelpful to me in these ways:

_____

_____

_____

_____

_____

_____

_____

... and more to do

Think about how ADHD makes your life harder or more challenging. Check off all the things that apply to you, and use the blank lines to add others. Note that the top half includes how ADHD impacts your life in general, while the bottom half includes how it impacts your feelings.

☐ Am easily distracted

☐ Don't get work done on time

☐ Lose things I need

☐ Struggle to concentrate long enough to finish tasks

☐ Forget to do what I'm supposed to

☐ Get yelled at a lot

☐ Lose track of time

☐ Don't keep my stuff organized

☐ Can't sit still long enough to get work done

☐ Miss what the teacher said—my mind is elsewhere

☐ Give up too soon or sometimes even before I start

☐ Annoy family and classmates with my hyperactive behavior

☐ Work twice as hard as my friends

☐ Say things without thinking

☐ Make poor choices—don't think about consequences

☐ Have trouble calming my brain down

☐ Worry that I'm not good enough

☐ Don't know what's going on

☐ Other: _____

☐ Other: _____

☐ Other: _____

☐ Anxious

☐ Frustrated

☐ Feel like a failure

☐ Discouraged

☐ Angry

☐ Confused

☐ Stressed

☐ Afraid

☐ Ashamed

☐ Other: _____

☐ Other: _____

☐ Other: _____

ADHD author Lara Honos-Webb encourages teens to think about ADHD as a gift in their lives. With that idea in mind, spend a few minutes considering the things you like about having ADHD. Check all those that apply. For each one you checked, write in a specific example from your life. Keep a copy of this list handy so you can look at it when you are having a bad day to remind yourself of the positive aspects of having ADHD.

☐ Creativity: _____

_____

☐ Having lots of ideas: _____

_____

☐ Having lots of energy: _____

_____

☐ Enthusiasm: _____

_____

☐ Spontaneity: _____

_____

☐ Quick thinking: _____

_____

☐ Fun: _____

_____

☐ Being smart: _____

_____

☐ Thinking outside the box: _____

_____

☐ Hyperfocus: _____

_____

☐ Leadership: _____

_____

☐ Other: _____

☐ Other: _____

☐ Other: _____

what do you need 3
help with?

for you to know

Everyone could use some help sometimes, so don't be embarrassed to ask for it. There are a lot of resources available to help you thrive with ADHD. Being mindful of how ADHD impacts your life helps you identify areas where you might benefit from some support. Then you can ask for the help you need.

When Billy became more mindful of how ADHD impacted his life, he noticed some things he had been struggling with almost every day. He made a list of areas where he needed help. Since he had trouble organizing his homework papers and keeping track of when his assignments were due, he asked for help with organizational skills and learned to use an app on his phone that really helped him turn in his assignments on time.

He also struggled to get along with his classmates and wished he had more friends. He joined a social skills group at school and learned some basic skills for connecting and interacting more successfully with his peers.

Billy knew he was on the right track when he turned in all his math homework on time and got a better grade on his math test. And he felt more accepted when a classmate sat with him at lunch and invited him to a party.

for you to do

Think about the areas where you struggle to succeed. Make a list of things you need help with. Be specific. (Examples: keeping track of assignments, getting my homework done and turned in on time, making friends, practicing for a job interview)

I need help with:

_____

_____

_____

_____

_____

_____

_____

_____

Find out where you can get the help you need. Write down what you need help with and where you can get it. Be specific. If you don't know where to get help, ask your parents, school guidance counselor or social worker, therapist, or teacher. These other sources may also be able to help:

- Study skills class
- Social skills group
- Tutor
- ADHD coach
- Job coach
- Friends
- Other family members

What I Need Help With	Who Can Help

Remember, everyone needs help sometimes. Asking for it will make your life easier and help you succeed with less stress.

... and more to do

Make a commitment to take the first step toward getting help. Write down the two most important things you need help with, and list who and when you will ask for help.

1. I need help with _____

    I will ask these resources for help: _____

    _____

    I will contact them by this date: _____

2. I need help with _____

    I will ask these resources for help: _____

    _____

    I will contact them by this date: _____

setting your intention 4

for you to know

You will be more successful at the things you want to master and achieve if you set an intention of what you want to accomplish before you start. An intention is something you plan to do. Once you are clear about your intention, you can set goals that align with it. This helps you stay focused and on task, and finish what you set out to do.

When John sat down to do his homework, he was usually distracted by noises in the room, his phone, stuff on his desk, and often by his own daydreams. He would lose his train of thought and have to figure out where he had left off when he got distracted. It felt like it took forever to finish each assignment.

John's therapist told him about setting an intention, which was a basic process in mindfulness that could help him stay on task. She told him that when you set your intention you simply decide what you will pay attention to. Then as soon as you notice you are paying attention to something else instead, you can remind yourself to bring your attention back to its intended focus.

She suggested that he start by asking himself these questions before he began an activity or started working toward something:

- *Why do I want to do this?*

- *What will I accomplish?*

- *What is the purpose of this intention?*

John agreed to try setting his intention to stay focused on his homework before starting his homework. He started on the first math problem and soon noticed that he was fiddling with the paper clip on his paper. He reminded himself of his intention to pay attention to his homework. Then he told himself, Not now, *and brought his attention back to the math problem.*

When he first tried this, he noticed that he was distracted over and over again, but he stayed calm and just brought his attention back to his homework each time. With practice, he realized he was getting his homework done faster than ever. Even though he still got distracted, he became quicker at noticing it and bringing his attention back to his homework.

He tried setting an intention when he was talking with Lily, a girl he thought was cute, to pay attention to her eyes and the sound of her voice. Every time he noticed he was looking around the room or thinking about his upcoming ball game, he reminded himself of his intention, brought his focus back to Lily's eyes, and tuned back in to what she was saying to him. When he did this, he realized that he heard more of what she said and remembered it better. And he discovered that Lily wanted to talk to him more often than ever.

for you to do

Study these three examples of setting intentions, and use what you learn to set your own intentions.

1. Intention: I intend to pay attention to the teacher in class.

    Why do I want to do this?

    *   My grades need to be better for me to get into college.

    *   I never know what my homework is.

    *   I don't understand the material.

    What will I accomplish?

    *   I will stay better focused.

    *   I won't daydream as much.

    *   I will avoid distraction.

    *   I will understand the material presented in class.

    *   I will be able to participate in class discussion.

    *   I will know what my homework is.

    What is the purpose of this intention?

    *   Getting better grades

    *   Feeling better about myself

    *   Getting schoolwork done on time

    *   Being prepared to get into college

2. Intention: I will set my alarm to beep every ten minutes when I am doing homework. That's how long I know I can concentrate.

    Why do I want to do this?

    *   I lose focus after about ten minutes and this will help me get back on task.

    *   I want to get my homework done more quickly.

What will I accomplish?

* I will bring my attention back to my homework more quickly.

* I will get my homework done faster.

* I will avoid getting sidetracked when I get distracted.

What is the purpose of this intention?

* Getting better grades

* Finishing my homework without getting so distracted

3. Intention: I will pay better attention to driving whenever I drive.

Why do I want to do this?

* My parents will let me drive their car if I pay better attention.

* My parents might trust me to drive safely with a friend in the car.

What will I accomplish?

* I will avoid accidents.

* I won't get lost.

* I will be allowed to borrow the car more often.

What is the purpose of this intention?

* Being a safe driver

* Being responsible

Now, check off any examples of intentions you have:

☐ I intend to pay attention to the teacher in class.

☐ I intend to get a better grade in _____.

☐ I intend to turn in all my homework.

☐ I intend to ask for help in my _____ class.

☐ I intend to be a safe driver.

☐ I intend to be a good friend.

☐ I intend to help out around the house.

☐ I intend to ask _____ to the prom.

☐ I intend to hang out with _____ when my homework is done.

☐ I intend to get into a good college.

☐ I intend to get on the varsity _____ team.

☐ I intend to get more sleep.

☐ I intend to get to school on time today.

☐ I intend to get a part-time job at _____.

☐ I intend to notice when I am hyper and calm myself down.

☐ I intend to be kinder to my sister or brother.

☐ I intend to stop and think about the consequences before I say or do something impulsively.

Write down any other intentions you have:

_____

_____

_____

_____

_____

Rank your intentions in order of priority. Place a "1" by the most important, a "2" by the next most important, and so on. Make a list of the top five, and post it on your bedroom door, bathroom mirror, or somewhere you will see it every day to remind yourself of your intention.

... and more to do

For practice, answer the prompts below for your top five intentions. Each time you set out to do something, repeat this process until it becomes a habit and you can set your intention automatically without having to write it all down. Whenever you realize you are off task, remind yourself of your intention, and bring your focus back in line with that intention.

Intention: _____

_____

Why do I want to do this? _____

_____

_____

What will I accomplish? _____

_____

_____

What is the purpose of this intention? _____

_____

_____

Make copies of this page and use it for each of your intentions until you routinely do this process automatically without having to write it down. Visit http://www.newharbinger .com/36255 to download a blank form you can use to do this activity.

Section 2

Mindfulness at Home and School

Teens with ADHD often struggle with poor concentration and organization, as well as anxiety and hyperactivity that can make it hard to do well in school and contribute to family life at home. This section provides mindfulness skills that help you organize your space and your schoolwork, get things done faster, improve your concentration, take tests with less anxiety, calm hyperactivity, and understand how you contribute to your family.

5 mindfulness of your contribution to the family

for you to know

Teens are normally expected to help out around the house and to contribute to family life in various ways. When you have ADHD, you may have difficulty completing chores, keeping your belongings organized, and getting things done. Understanding your role in your family and being mindful of what your parents expect of you will help you stay motivated and get things done.

Fifteen-year-old Jason had ADHD and felt like he was always getting yelled at when he was home. It seemed like nothing he did around the house was ever good enough for his parents. They didn't like his messy room. They complained that he never got his chores done. Sometimes he forgot to feed the dog. He just wanted to play video games or text his friends when he got home from school, but his parents wanted him to get his homework done, take out the garbage, and keep his room tidy. When he tried to do everything they wanted, he usually got distracted and forgot what he was doing. Then he wouldn't finish what he was supposed to do. He didn't understand why he had to do everything anyway.

When Jason learned about the importance of his role in his family, he started to pay attention to how he could contribute by doing his chores so his family members would all feel better and have more time to have fun. He realized that he was an important member of the family and that his parents depended on him to do his share. He found out that his mother felt like he didn't care about her when he ignored her requests, and this made them both feel bad. He discovered that when he really understood what his parents expected of him, he felt more motivated to get the things done that they asked him to do. He noticed that he started feeling better about himself, and he felt more like a part of the family.

for you to do

Spend a few minutes thinking about what your parents expect of you. This will help you be more aware of what your role is in your family and how you can contribute to family life. It may help you motivate yourself to do what you need to do and also help you feel more like you belong.

What do your parents expect of you? Check all that apply. Add other things at the bottom.

☐ Keep my room clean

☐ Do my laundry

☐ Set and/or clear the table

☐ Load and/or empty the dishwasher

☐ Mow the lawn

☐ Vacuum

☐ Feed the dog or cat

☐ Get my homework done every night

☐ Cook a meal periodically

☐ Be respectful to them and to other people

☐ Be nice to my siblings

☐ Get good grades

☐ Behave appropriately

☐ Get a job

☐ Get into college

☐ Spend some time doing things with the family

☐ Hang out with friends they approve of

☐ Be responsible

☐ Do what I say I will do

☐ Tell the truth

☐ Let them know where I am

☐ Be home on time

☐ Follow the rules

☐ Listen when they talk to me

☐ Talk to them

☐ Let them know if I need help

☐ Never drink and drive

☐ Other: _____

☐ Other: _____

☐ Other: _____

Give three examples of what could happen if you didn't do what your parents expect you to do. (Examples: My cat is hungry because I didn't feed it; my parents get angry when I forget to mow the lawn which now looks bad and is harder to mow; I get in trouble for drinking at friend's party.)

1. _____

2. _____

3. _____

... and more to do

There are many ways to contribute to your family at home. (Examples: do my chores, plan a fun activity, play with my brothers or sisters, help my brother or sister with homework, help my parents do something, talk to my parents about my life, join in family recreation, get my homework done without my parents needing to nag at me, teach my family something I am learning about at school, bring my friends home, do something with my parent [such as shopping, fishing, running, home repair], tell my parents about my day, help my grandparents, talk to my parents about my concerns about topics like the environment, poverty, or war)

Write down ten ways you can or do contribute to your family:

1. _____

2. _____

3. _____

4. _____

5. _____

6. _____

7. _____

8. _____

9. _____

10._____

Post this list where you can see it every day to remind you to be mindful of your contribution. Visit http://www.newharbinger.com/36255 to download a blank form you can fill out and post.

6   organizing your space

for you to know

Teens with ADHD typically have trouble organizing their things and their space. You can learn to be more organized by setting up a system for where everything goes and becoming mindful of putting things back where they belong. Although this sounds like more work, it will actually make your life easier and much less stressful.

Jake was always losing things. He spent a lot of time trying to find his clothes, his homework, and his belongings. He felt frustrated and angry when he was late because he was looking for something he needed. He was embarrassed when he didn't do his homework because he had lost it, sometimes even after he had already done it. When he was using something, he often put it down without paying attention to where he put it or where it was supposed to go. As a result, his room was a disaster, his backpack was a mess, his locker was totally unusable, and his grades were suffering. And he felt stressed!

Jake decided to become more mindful about where he put his things. He realized that he rarely put things away and often didn't even know where they belonged. He spent an afternoon cleaning out his room, throwing out things he no longer needed, removing things that didn't belong in his room, and finding a place to put everything. He set an alarm to remind him each evening to spend five minutes putting things away in his room. Then he developed a habit of cleaning out his backpack once a week and taking out anything that did not need to be taken back and forth to school every day. He set an alarm on his phone calendar to remind him to empty out his locker at the end of each Friday and to arrange his books so he could find them quickly between classes.

Now that everything in his room had a home and he knew where things belonged, he found it easier to put things away. Having his alarm remind him to spend five minutes each night putting things away kept things from getting out of control, and he stopped feeling so overwhelmed when he walked into his room. He even started putting his clothes right into the hamper when he got undressed instead of dropping them on the floor, which saved him from having to pick them up again later.

for you to do

Too much stuff creates a chaotic space that can feel overwhelming. Use this process to keep your bedroom, backpack, and locker cleaned out and organized.

1. Get three large bags.

2. Gather trash and place it in the first bag to throw away.

3. Remove anything that doesn't belong, and place it in the second bag to find a new home.

4. Place things you no longer need or use in the third bag to donate or hand down.

5. Make a list of items that do belong and write down where they go.

6. Put each item where it belongs.

7. Post the list where you can see it.

8. Make it a habit to put things where they belong every day.

9. Use labels to remind you where things go.

Here's what the process might look like if you were organizing your bedroom:

1. Bring three bags to your room.

2. Put trash in the first bag.

3. Remove things that don't belong in your bedroom and place them in the second bag. Be mindful of the fact that your bedroom is primarily for sleeping and getting dressed. Think about what else you currently use your bedroom for, such as eating, doing homework, playing video games, or watching TV. If you have trouble sleeping, remove anything that activates your brain—for example, your phone, games, activities, and homework—and find a place outside the bedroom to do these activities. Take food and dirty dishes to the kitchen. Fill the second bag with items to store elsewhere.

4. Get rid of things you no longer need or use. Put them in the third bag to donate or hand down.

5. Take this worksheet into your bedroom. Make a list of items in the room, and write down where they belong (for example, shirts–second drawer, jeans–hanging in closet,

dirty clothes–hamper, backpack–by my desk, shoes–bottom of closet on shoe rack). Use a second sheet of paper, if needed.

6. Put each item where it belongs.

7. Post this list somewhere in your bedroom to remind you where things belong.

8. Refer to this list daily until putting things away becomes a habit.

9. Using your list as a guide, put labels on drawers and shelves to remind you where things go.

Item	Where It Belongs

Visit http://www.newharbinger.com/36255 to download a blank form to fill out and post.

... and more to do

Set your intention to be mindful of keeping your bedroom, backpack, and locker neat and organized by completing the following statements with the date or day of the week you will do each one. Remember that most of them need to be done at least once a week.

I plan to clean out and organize my bedroom on _____ (date).

I plan to clean out and organize my backpack on _____ (date).

I plan to clean out and organize my locker on _____ (date).

I will remove things from my bedroom that don't belong there every _____ (day).

I will remove things from my backpack that don't belong there every _____ (day).

I will remove things from my locker that don't belong there every _____ (day).

I will remove things from my bedroom that I no longer need or use every _____ (day).

I will remove things from my backpack that I no longer need or use every _____ (day).

I will remove things from my locker that I no longer need or use every _____ (day).

I will find a place for each item that belongs in my bedroom every _____ (day).

I will find a place for each item that belongs in my backpack every _____ (day).

I will find a place for each item that belongs in my locker every _____ (day).

I will put everything away where it belongs every _____ (day).

I intend to put things away every day at this time: _____

I set my alarm for _____ o'clock to remind me to put things away daily.

Now that you have completed this, add each task with an alarm on your calendar app or reminder app on your phone or on your paper calendar or planner to remind you to do them.

7 getting things done on time

for you to know

Because teens with ADHD are often easily distracted, they can have difficulty getting things done on time. Some struggle with having an appropriate sense of time and therefore don't realize how much time has passed. Being mindful of what needs to be done and by when will help you stay on schedule.

Hannah felt frustrated because she was almost always late. Everything she did seemed to take longer than it should. She would start a task and soon discover that she was doing something unrelated, or that she had been distracted by her own thoughts and now she was behind. This was a source of embarrassment for her, and she wished she could get things done on time.

Hannah wanted to get things done more quickly. She learned to use a mindful process that helped her break tasks into small, manageable pieces that helped her stay focused. One day when she had homework, she wrote down the three most important things she needed to get done, which were her math, social studies, and science assignments. Then she picked the most pressing, which was her math homework because it was due tomorrow and she thought it would take the most time.

She broke this first task into small segments (a few math problems) that could each be done in a short amount of time. She set her intention to pay attention to the first set of problems. She thought she should be able to finish the first segment of the task (the first set of problems) in about fifteen minutes, so she set an alarm for fifteen minutes and started working. As soon as she noticed that her mind had wandered, she brought her attention back to the task and reminded herself she wanted to finish it within fifteen minutes.

She kept doing this over and over until the alarm sounded. She realized she needed just a few more minutes to complete the first set, so she set the alarm for four more minutes and brought her attention back to her work. When she finished the set, she took a short break and then repeated the process with the next segment of the task (the next set of problems) until all the problems were done. Then she used the same process on the second most important task on her list, which was to read a chapter in her social studies book.

With practice, Hannah noticed that she was getting things done faster because she wasn't distracted for as long as she used to be.

for you to do

Write down the tasks that you often have trouble getting done on time (Examples: homework, exams, chores, getting ready in the morning, getting to school):

_____

_____

_____

_____

_____

What gets in your way of getting things done on time?

_____

_____

_____

_____

When you need to get something done, use the following process until you can do it automatically without writing everything down:

1. List three important tasks you need to do. Include when they must be done by.

    _____

    _____

    _____

2. Choose the most important task to start with and write it here: _____

3. How can you break this task into small, manageable segments?

    _____

    _____

    _____

4. List everything you need to complete the task and gather it before you start.

_____

_____

_____

_____

5. Set your intention of what you want to pay attention to in order to complete the first segment of the task. Write it down here:

_____

_____

6. How long do you think the first segment of the task should take? _____ Set an alarm or timer for that time.

7. Start doing the task. When you notice you are off task, imagine pushing your reset button and bring your attention back to the task.

8. If you are not done when the alarm sounds, see how much you have left to do and reset the alarm or timer for that time.

9. Do steps 4–8 for each segment of the task.

10. Repeat steps 2–9 for each task.

... and more to do

Now that you have practiced this process with a few tasks, reflect on what happened when you did it.

What's the most important task you did? _____

How did you decide how to break it into segments? _____

How did you feel doing each smaller segment compared to how you usually feel doing the entire task?

_____

_____

Did focusing on one segment of the task make it easier to stay on task? (Y/N)

Did you get the whole task done? (Y/N)

What, if anything, would you do differently next time to make this work the best for you?

_____

_____

_____

What tasks that you need to do regularly will you use this process for?

_____

_____

8 how long can you stay on task?

for you to know

Having ADHD can make it harder to stay on task and finish things on time. When you know how long you can pay attention, you can break your tasks into smaller chunks of time that make it easier to stay on task. Also, when you are aware of the things that typically distract you, you can find ways to eliminate or avoid them while doing tasks.

Cameron struggled to get his homework done. He was easily distracted and often felt so overwhelmed by the thought of doing his homework that he procrastinated and avoided doing it—often until it was too late to get it done at all. Sometimes he felt like such a failure. He started to believe that he couldn't concentrate at all.

With his guidance counselor's help, he realized that he actually could concentrate but not for very long. His counselor helped him figure out how long he could focus and taught him a technique he could use to break his work into time segments that did not exceed his ideal focusing time. He was able to accomplish more in each segment and started feeling better about himself.

for you to do

Let's figure out how long you can stay focused.

- When you start doing your homework, start the timer on your phone.

- As soon as you notice that you are not paying attention to your homework, stop the timer.

- Write down how long you paid attention.

- Repeat this ten times.

- Add up all the times you wrote down, and divide by ten to get the average time you are able to stay focused. This is your ideal focusing time.

Now that you know how long you can stay focused, break the tasks you need to do into chunks that take about that long to complete.

- Set a timer for your ideal focusing time when you start a task, and take a short break when the timer sounds.

- Then reset the timer and do the next part of the task.

- Repeat this process until the task is complete.

After you have practiced this process, set the timer for a minute longer than your current ideal focusing time, and see if you can stay focused until the timer sounds. This will gradually help you increase the time you can stay focused.

... and more to do

Your ability to stay focused may vary depending on internal factors such as your mood; how tired you are; how stressed you feel; how antsy, hyper, or revved up you feel; and how difficult you feel the task is that you are doing. Make a list of the internal factors you have noticed that affect your ability to concentrate.

_____

_____

_____

_____

Write down what you can do to prepare yourself to be able to concentrate. (Examples: get a good night's sleep, eat a healthy snack, go for a run [or other exercise] before doing homework, calm your body, relax your mind, practice de-stressing techniques, clear your mind) Note that many skills from later in the book will support you in preparing to concentrate.

_____

_____

_____

_____

are you hyperactive? 9

for you to know

Teens with the hyperactive/impulsive type of ADHD are often unusually physically active or hyperactive. Being aware of your hyperactivity can help you manage it and channel your energy so it doesn't interfere with completing tasks. What's more, your hyperactivity will be less annoying to others.

Brendan was always in motion, but he didn't notice when he moved more than other teens. His parents, teachers, and even his friends often said, "Sit still, Brendan" or "Chill out." His parents sometimes told him his constant fidgeting and finger tapping was driving them crazy. He had trouble sitting still long enough to get through class or to get his homework done. He felt best when he could go for a run outside or lift weights before he had to sit still.

Brendan's therapist suggested that he tune into his hyperactivity. She explained that by becoming more aware of it and how it impacted his life and those around him, he might then be able to apply some techniques to calm his body down when he needed to do so. She said that there was nothing wrong with being hyper—and in fact it could help him concentrate because it may indirectly activate the attention center in the brain—but she wondered if it sometimes got in the way of his success.

for you to do

The first step in managing hyperactivity is to become aware of it. Notice if you have any of these signs of hyperactivity, and also ask your parents, friends, and teachers if they have noticed you doing any of these. Check off those that apply to you.

- ☐ Constantly moving
- ☐ Fidgeting
- ☐ Finger tapping
- ☐ Foot tapping
- ☐ Leg swinging
- ☐ Trouble sitting still
- ☐ Lots of energy
- ☐ Feeling antsy
- ☐ Jumpiness
- ☐ Restlessness
- ☐ Talking excessively
- ☐ Easily bored
- ☐ Racing thoughts
- ☐ Pacing
- ☐ Can't relax
- ☐ Feeling wired

List five things you like about being hyperactive.

1. _____
2. _____
3. _____
4. _____
5. _____

List five ways being hyperactive gets in the way of your success.

1. _____
2. _____
3. _____
4. _____
5. _____

List three ways being hyperactive has helped you get something done.

1. _____
2. _____
3. _____

List three times your hyperactivity helped you concentrate.

1. _____
2. _____
3. _____

activity 9 ✳ are you hyperactive?

List three times your hyperactivity annoyed someone. Include who it annoyed.

1. _____

2. _____

3. _____

List three times you noticed you were hyperactive today. Where were you, and what were you doing?

1. _____

2. _____

3. _____

List three times you noticed your body was calm today. Where were you and what were you doing?

1. _____

2. _____

3. _____

You can learn to calm down your body any time you notice that you are hyperactive. Practice using the following brief meditation to tune in and calm your body.

Remove distractions and find a comfortable position.

Tune in to your body.

Notice how your body feels. Is it calm or restless? Still or moving?

Does it feel warm or cold? Loose or tight? Light or heavy?

Slowly take a deep breath in through your nose, and imagine filling your body with a cushion of relaxing air that soothes, warms, and calms your body.

Now gently breathe out like you are blowing a giant bubble, and as you do so, imagine letting go of any excess activity in your body.

Let it go. You just don't need it right now.

Do it again.

Notice any areas of your body that feel restless or are moving.

Take a slow, gentle breath in through your nose and fill those areas of your body with calming energy.

Breathe out even more slowly through your mouth, and imagine all the excess physical energy or activity in your body slowly flowing out of you.

Repeat this while taking three more slow and gentle breaths.

Practice this technique three times each day; for example, before you get out of bed in the morning, when you take a shower, and before you fall asleep. Then use it any time you notice you are feeling very restless or are having trouble sitting still.

Visit http://www.newharbinger.com/36255 to download an audio version of this brief meditation, and listen to it whenever you feel hyper or antsy until you can use the process on your own to calm your body.

... and more to do

Physical exercise increases your awareness of your body, boosts attention, improves your mood, reduces impulsivity, and uses up extra energy. In addition, being outside in nature can calm you down.

Write down when you will get some exercise every day to burn off excess energy.

_____

_____

Write down when you can spend a few minutes every day outside in nature.

_____

_____

Practice the following steps to challenge yourself to lie still. This will increase your awareness of your body and practice keeping it still.

1. Gather six coins or chips from a board game.

2. Lie down on your back on your bed or on the floor.

3. One by one, place the coins or chips on your thighs, shoulders, forehead, and chin.

4. Now pay attention to how they feel as you lie perfectly still and balance them on your body.

5. See how long you can lie still before you move and knock one off.

6. Practice this daily and notice whether you can lie still a little longer each day.

If you are having trouble sitting still during the day, close your eyes for a moment and imagine how it felt when you were balancing the coins or chips. Does this help you calm down your body?

you can improve your 10
concentration

for you to know

ADHD makes it difficult to pay attention. You can improve your concentration when you practice noticing when you are distracted and refocusing your attention. This helps you effectively rewire your brain by training it to be more efficient. Then it is easier to concentrate for longer periods of time.

Jennifer had so much trouble concentrating that she often didn't get her classwork done in time. She hated the fact that it took her hours to do homework that her friends did in less than half the time. And she often forgot where she put things and didn't do what her parents asked her to do, simply because she wasn't paying attention when she put things down or when her parents told her what they wanted her to do. She was beginning to feel like a failure and worried that she wouldn't earn good enough grades or do well enough on her entrance exams to get into college. She wished she could learn to concentrate better.

Jennifer's ADHD coach taught her some skills designed to reduce distractions and increase her ability to concentrate. Jennifer was very skeptical about how the skills would work, but she agreed to give them a try. At first it was hard to do them. Her coach reassured her that she was learning a new skill that was teaching her brain to concentrate better and that it was normal for her thoughts to wander. When she stuck with the process of bringing her attention back to the task at hand, she noticed that it was getting a little easier. She was delighted that after a few weeks of practice she noticed it was easier to concentrate and she was getting her homework done faster. She finally felt hopeful that she would get into college and be successful after all.

for you to do

Teens with ADHD are often distracted by things around them and have trouble concentrating long enough to get things done on time. Noticing what diverts your attention can help you eliminate many distractions and find ways to handle those you cannot eliminate.

Make a list of the things outside of you that distract you. Include where you are and what you are doing when they distract you.

_____

_____

_____

_____

_____

_____

Using the list above, write down five ways you can eliminate, avoid, or handle things that distract you when you need to concentrate. (Examples: use headphones, listen to classical music to block out the noise in your house when you are doing your homework, turn off your phone while you do your chores or your homework, turn off the TV when you need to focus on homework, turn on the TV if that helps you stay on task as it does for some, put the dog in its crate so it doesn't keep trying to get you to play)

1. _____

2. _____

3. _____

4. _____

5. _____

... and more to do

When you need to concentrate on a task such as homework, a test, or a chore, use the following mindfulness-of-tasks process to stay focused.

1. Choose the task you need to do and set your intention to pay attention to that task.

2. Pay attention to that specific task and concentrate on doing it.

3. Observe when your mind has wandered and you are no longer paying attention to your intended task.

4. Let go of the distracted thought.

5. Refocus your attention to your intended task.

6. Repeat steps 2–5 until the task is done.

Pick a task, such as brushing your teeth, and practice the process every day for a week. Then pick another task, such as doing your math homework, and follow the process while you do that task. Keep practicing until it becomes second nature.

This short acronym can help you remember the steps in this process: iPOLAR (sort of like iPhone or iPad).

Set your **i**ntention

Pay attention

Observe distracted thought

Let it go

And

Refocus

In order to stay focused, use the following distraction-delay skill to avoid engaging with distracting thoughts.

- Keep a blank piece of paper and a pen handy, or use the notes or reminder app on your phone.

- When you are working on a task and notice you are being distracted by a thought that is not about that task or by something in your environment, write down the thought or distraction or type it into your phone. Say to yourself, *Not now, maybe later,* then bring your attention back to your intended task.

- Repeat this process every time you notice you are off task, until the task is completed.

- Once the task is done, look at the list you made and see if there is anything on it that you need to pay attention to, and repeat the process with this task when appropriate.

organizing your schoolwork 11

for you to know

Teens with ADHD find it difficult to organize their schoolwork and keep track of their assignments. You can create and use a system to keep your papers and assignments organized so you won't lose homework or forget to do assignments.

Zach wasn't doing as well in school as he wanted to. He had a hard time organizing his homework assignments and getting things turned in on time. He often felt anxious about school and embarrassed when he didn't know what his assignments were and then fell behind. Sometimes he lost his homework even after he had spent hours doing it. Often he felt like giving up and didn't bother to do his homework. He wondered if he was stupid, but he knew deep inside that he was smart and that he could get better grades if he could just keep track of his homework.

Zach's teacher showed him a system for keeping track of what his assignments were and when they were due. Then she showed him how to organize his papers. It took some practice to use the system, but when he did, he knew what his assignments were and he got them done on time. He noticed that he felt better about school and wasn't as anxious anymore. Feeling better helped him motivate himself to use the system.

for you to do

Let's find out if you need help with organizing your schoolwork. Check off all that apply to you.

☐ I forget to write down homework assignments and when they are due.

☐ I often don't know what my assignments are.

☐ I fall behind on my homework.

☐ I lose points on my grades because I don't turn my homework in.

☐ I often lose my homework even after I have completed it.

☐ I feel anxious about school because I am behind.

☐ Sometimes I stay home from school because I am not prepared for a test or a project.

How are you keeping track of your assignments and when they are due now?

_____

_____

… and more to do

You can use mindfulness and organizational skills to succeed at getting your homework done on time and turning it in. Read the following steps aloud, and then practice doing each step until they become habits. Notice how much easier it is to keep your homework organized when you follow these steps.

- I will explore options for keeping track of what my assignments are and when they are due. I will:

  * ask my teacher for a recommendation;

  * search online for a homework app and find one I can use on my phone;

  * find and use an assignment book; and

  * see if assignments are available online at my school's website.

- Before I leave each class I will write down or enter my assignment and when it is due. If I often forget to do this, I will set an alarm on my phone to remind me.

- I will break large projects into small pieces and enter when I should have each piece done into my assignment book or app.

- I will use pocket folders, with a different color for each class.

- When a homework paper is assigned, I will place it in the right-hand pocket of the folder for that class.

- When I sit down to do my homework, I will read over my assignments and note when they are due.

- I will choose the homework that is due first and take out the materials I need to do that homework.

- I will do the homework for one class at a time, and when I am done I will put the homework to be turned in inside the left-hand pocket on the folder for that class.

- I will keep all the folders in a homework binder.

- I will place graded homework in a folder for each class so I can refer to it when I study.

- I will ask my school for a second set of textbooks that I can keep at home so I always have the books I need.

- When all my homework is done, I will place my folders and homework binder in my backpack and place it by the door before I go to bed.

- I will set my calendar alarm on my phone to remind me to clean out my backpack once a week.

Visit http://www.newharbinger.com/36255 to download a copy of these steps. Print it out and post it where you can refer to it easily.

calming your test anxiety 12

for you to know

Many teens with ADHD often worry that they will be distracted while taking a test and then won't finish it on time. This can cause test anxiety and stress, which makes it even harder to do well. You can prepare yourself ahead of time to head off this kind of anxiety so you can stay calm and focused while taking a test.

Ashley dreaded taking tests. She noticed that she often felt stressed and anxious whenever she thought about school. Sometimes her stomach hurt so much on the day a test was scheduled that she stayed home from school. But she had to take the test sometime.

Her therapist suggested she use some mindfulness skills to help her prepare for tests and to calm her anxiety. Ashley noticed that when she was able to study for each test while remaining calm, she felt more confident about doing well. Whenever she noticed she was feeling anxious, she practiced a simple breathing technique that helped her stay calm.

for you to do

Do you have test anxiety? Check off all that apply to you, and use the blank lines to add any others.

☐ I often feel overwhelmed and worry about how I'm going to do on a test.

☐ I get symptoms of anxiety, such as headache, dry mouth, rapid heartbeat, sweating, shortness of breath, nausea, diarrhea, or feeling too hot or cold.

☐ I procrastinate when I need to study.

☐ I second-guess myself, change my answers, or get stuck.

☐ I have more trouble concentrating when I worry about how I'm doing.

☐ My thoughts are negative and predict the worst; for example, *I will fail, so why bother even trying?*

☐ Other: _____

☐ Other: _____

If you've checked off any of these, you will benefit from strategies to reduce test anxiety.

... and more to do

Prevent and reduce test anxiety by taking these steps.

Before the test:

- Put the exam on your assignment calendar.
- Plan ahead to leave yourself plenty of time to study.
- Build confidence by studying for the exam.
- Ask a friend or family member to quiz you.
- Create a game plan for taking the test.
- Give yourself a practice test, time yourself, and try to mimic the test situation to get used to it.
- Get enough sleep the night before.
- Get some exercise an hour before the test.

During the test:

- Use accommodations your school allows for students with ADHD, such as extra time for the exam or taking it in a less distracting place.
- Answer multiple-choice questions as quickly as possible; make notes about those you have doubt about and go back to them later.
- If you notice that you are experiencing anxiety, follow these steps:
  - * To the count of four, breathe calm and safety in through your nose.
  - * To the count of eight, breathe worry and stress out through your mouth.
  - * Say to yourself, *I am prepared. I can do this.* (Repeat three times every time you notice you feel anxious.)
  - * Envision success.
  - * Bring your attention back to the test.

If you find this checklist helpful, you can print it out or save it on your phone and use it anytime you have a test to prepare for. Visit http://www.newharbinger.com/36255 to download a copy.

Section 3

Getting Along with Yourself and Others

Teens with ADHD often feel stressed, frustrated, and discouraged when they don't do as well as they want to despite trying really hard. The activities in this section help you de-stress, find thoughts that feel better, and be less hard on yourself. They also help you get along more easily with family and friends.

13 how's your mood today?

for you to know

Teens often experience intense emotions that can change suddenly and dramatically. This can feel like an emotional roller coaster. ADHD often makes these feelings even more intense. The first step in managing and regulating your emotions is to become aware of how you are feeling and to name the feeling. Then you can use practical mindfulness skills to quickly shift your mood and feel better.

Tyler noticed that he sometimes felt like he was on top of the world, but all too often he felt easily annoyed, irritated, angry, stressed, depressed, or worried. He wondered if it was normal to feel so intensely and for his mood to change so quickly. Often, he was not even sure what he was feeling.

His therapist assured him that it is normal for teens to have intense and changeable emotions, and that having ADHD often makes it worse. She taught him some mindfulness skills to help him notice his mood and then to gently change it for the better.

At first, Tyler found it difficult to tune in to his emotions. With practice, he got better at noticing and identifying how he was feeling. He was amazed at how his emotions always seemed to show up in his body somewhere. He quickly discovered that he could change his mood and experience contentment and gratitude by simply remembering a time he felt grateful.

for you to do

We all have feelings or emotions throughout the day. These often come and go, only to be replaced with new emotions. You can become more mindful of your emotions by following these steps:

Take a moment to stop what you are doing and tune in.

Take some time to pay attention to your breathing; just notice your breathing without changing it.

Notice how you are feeling.

Identify the feeling—name it. Are you happy, sad, worried, calm, excited, relaxed, curious, proud, irritated, angry, stressed, content?

Notice how and where the feeling shows up in your body. Are your muscles tense? Does your stomach or head ache?

Is there any part of your body that feels uncomfortable?

Observe the feeling.

Does it feel good, bad, or neither good nor bad?

Is it coming and going or staying steady?

Is it changing?

When have you felt this way before?

Accept the feeling. Don't judge it or try to change it; just let it be for now.

Investigate the present moment of the feeling.

Notice the part of the emotion that has to do with the present, as well as the past or future aspects of the feeling.

Stay focused on the part of the emotion that has to do with the present.

Don't identify with the feeling. You have a feeling. Your feeling does not equal who you are.

What are the thoughts and the story behind the feeling?

What caused you to feel this way?

What unhelpful emotion can you replace with a helpful one? For example, you could replace sadness with hope or worry with calmness.

Bring your attention to your breath.

Reflect on what came up for you during this process.

Visit http://www.newharbinger.com/36255 to download an audio version of this process that you can use to tune in to your emotions.

... and more to do

Experiencing a feeling of gratitude and appreciation can help you shift out of an unhelpful emotion and feel happier. Practice doing the following process daily and whenever you are experiencing an unhelpful emotion. At http://www.newharbinger.com/36255, you can download a copy of these steps to write on.

Find a comfortable position. Tune in and notice how you feel.

Write down the name of the feeling. _____

Write down three things in your life that you are grateful for.

    1. _____

    2. _____

    3. _____

Write down three things that happened today that you appreciated.

    1. _____

    2. _____

    3. _____

Write down three people in your life that you appreciate.

    1. _____

    2. _____

    3. _____

Write a brief thank-you note to someone who has helped you in some way.

Dear _____,

Thank you for _____

_____

_____

If possible, give this person the thank-you note or read it out loud to him or her.

How does expressing gratitude make you feel?

_____

_____

Notice how you feel now.

Write down the name of the feeling and compare it to how you felt at the beginning of this exercise.

_____

_____

14 relaxation breath to calm and improve your mood

for you to know

You can calm and center yourself quickly by learning a breathing technique that quiets your mind and body. Then whenever you feel angry, anxious, stressed, or upset, you can use this technique to feel better fast.

Alex often felt stressed out. At those times, he noticed that his mind seemed to slow down or rev up too high, his thoughts were all over the place, and he couldn't think straight. Then he couldn't concentrate, make good choices, or get anything done, which caused even more stress.

His therapist taught him how to do a relaxation breath. She encouraged him to practice it several times every day, which was like pushing the reset button to lower his stress level. Then she suggested that he use it whenever he started to feel stressed, or when he really needed to calm down and focus on something like schoolwork. After he got the hang of it, he discovered that he could calm his mind and his body simply by breathing. He began to notice that he wasn't feeling so stressed anymore.

for you to do

You can calm down your mind and body by practicing a breathing technique called the relaxation breath. When you inhale, you activate yourself, and when you exhale, you calm yourself. Therefore, when you exhale twice as long as you inhale, your mind and body will relax. Practice the following breathing technique several times every day. Then use it to calm your mind and your body when you feel stressed, anxious, angry, or distracted. Do three or four relaxation breaths at a time and notice how much calmer your mind and body feel.

1. Stop what you are doing for a moment.

2. Tune in and notice how your mind and body feel.

3. Bring your attention to your breath.

4. Inhale slowly through your nose to the count of four.

5. Exhale even more slowly through your mouth to the count of eight, like you are blowing a huge bubble.

6. Do it again. Inhale to the count of four, and breathe in peace and relaxation.

7. Exhale to the count of eight, and relax your mind. Just let everything go that needs to go.

8. One more time, inhale to the count of four and breathe in a cushion of healing energy.

9. Now exhale to the count of eight and relax your body.

10. Now breathe normally.

11. Tune in to your mind and body and notice what has changed.

Visit http://www.newharbinger.com/36255 to download a version of this breathing technique.

... and more to do

The deeper you breathe, the more oxygen you send throughout your mind and body and the calmer you can become as you slowly exhale. Use the following technique to learn how to get a deep belly breath.

1. Place one hand on your chest.

2. Place the other hand on your belly, just below your rib cage.

3. Tune in and notice which hand is moving as you breathe normally.

4. If the hand on your chest moves more, that means you are chest breathing, which is shallow and stressful.

5. If the hand on your belly moves more, then you are belly breathing, which is deeper and more calming.

6. Take a chest breath and blow on your hand.

7. Now take a deep belly breath and blow on your hand.

8. When you take a belly breath, you may notice the air is warmer on your hand than from a chest breath.

9. Practice taking a belly breath until the air is warmer.

10. Place your hand on your belly.

11. Practice inhaling and imagine that you are inflating a balloon in your belly.

12. Feel your belly move as you inhale and then exhale.

13. Try lying on your back and place your cell phone or another small object on your belly.

14. Make the phone or other object move up and down as you breathe.

changing the channel on negative or anxious thoughts 15

for you to know

Many teens with ADHD develop a pattern of thinking negative or anxious thoughts. You may notice you have thoughts like these: *I will never get this done; No one will like me; I'm afraid I will fail; I'm not even going to try.* You can use a mindfulness skill to quickly change your "channel" from negative or anxious thoughts to a more positive and helpful "channel."

Kaylee was often very hard on herself. When her therapist encouraged her to pay attention to her self-talk, she noticed a constant barrage of anxious and negative statements that were usually putting herself down and often predicting the worst. She realized that she didn't feel very good when she thought this way.

Her therapist taught her a technique to change the "channel" on her negative and unhelpful thinking. First, she decided she would rather watch the happy or calm channel instead of the worried or negative channel. Then she picked a few things to put on each of these channels that made her feel calm or content. She always felt happy when she pictured her baby brother smiling at her, so she put his face on her happy channel. She remembered that she felt happy when she was at the lake so she also put a picture of the lake on her happy channel. She knew she felt calm when she looked at flowers in a garden, so she put flowers on her calm channel.

Each time she noticed that she was watching her worry channel, she pretended to pull her imaginary remote control from her pocket; she changed to her calm channel and visualized the flowers. She could feel herself calm down right away.

When she noticed she was watching her negative channel, she changed the channel in her mind to her happy channel with her baby brother's smiling face. This made her smile every time, and she instantly felt better. After a few weeks of practice, she noticed that her thoughts were staying more positive and helpful. She felt better just knowing she could quickly change the channel and feel better right away.

for you to do

Tuning in to what your thoughts are can be like noticing what channel you are watching on TV. If the channel you are watching doesn't help you feel good, you can change it to one that feels better.

What channel(s) do you "watch" in your thoughts?

- Take a moment to tune in and notice what you are thinking about.

    * What is the thought?

    * Is the thought helpful or unhelpful?

    * Is the thought negative, anxious, angry, or stressful?

    * Is the thought happy, positive, hopeful, or calm?

- As thoughts come and go, just keep noticing them.

- Are there any patterns to the thoughts?

- How do you feel when you think them?

- Name the channel(s) that you often watch in your mind. (Examples: worry, stress, distracted, all or nothing, predicting the worst)

    _____

    _____

- What channel(s) would you rather watch? (Examples: happy, hopeful, calm, relaxed, focused)

    _____

    _____

- List three things you would put on each of your channels.

    a. _____

    b. _____

    c. _____

- Spend a few minutes every day paying attention to what channel you are watching and noticing how you feel when you watch it.

- When you need to, you can easily change the channel.

  * Pretend to reach into your pocket, and pull out your imaginary remote control.

  * Change the channel to watch one of the channels you chose above, and imagine watching it for a few minutes.

  * Notice how you feel when you watch the new, more helpful channel.

... and more to do

When you notice that what you are thinking about is making you feel bad, down, anxious, or stressed, you can find a thought that feels better. It must be a thought that you can believe and that gives you a sense of relief when you think it. Here are some examples:

I'm stupid. Replace with: *I didn't do as well as I wanted on that test, but I got a good grade on my last test. I will study harder next time and work with my tutor.*

I'm so angry because I lost my homework. Replace with: *I lost my homework because I didn't put it in the folder where it belongs. Next time, I will remember to put it there. I will set an alarm on my phone to remind me.*

I'll never get this done in time. Replace with: *I have enough time. I just need to stay focused and breathe to calm myself down.*

I feel overwhelmed. Replace with: *I will break my schoolwork into small sections and focus on just one at a time until they are all done.*

No one likes me. Replace with: *Not everyone likes me, but Jess talked to me today, and I am getting better at talking with people.*

Write down an unhelpful thought that you often notice going through your head.

_____

_____

Write down a thought to replace this thought that you can believe and that feels better.

_____

_____

Repeat this process for three other thoughts.

Unhelpful thought: _____

_____

Replacement thought: _____

_____

Unhelpful thought: _____

_____

Replacement thought: _____

_____

Unhelpful thought: _____

_____

Replacement thought: _____

_____

Practice replacing unhelpful thoughts with helpful thoughts throughout your day.

Tell yourself, *Better but believable* as you find thoughts that feel better.

16 de-stressing instantly

for you to know

Life can be very stressful for a teen, and ADHD can multiply this stress. Sometimes you can simply decrease or remove the stressors. But when you can't, you can dial down your personal response to the stress by becoming mindful of it and using skills that calm your mind and body and refocus your attention.

Makayla often felt stressed out and overwhelmed. She knew that not all stress is bad and that it could help to keep her safe and at her peak. But chronic stress was draining Makayla's energy and making her feel anxious and depressed. After her therapist helped her identify and list the sources of stress in her life (the stressors), she made some changes that decreased the stress. This helped a lot. She was able to eliminate the stress of not having the right textbook at home to do her homework by getting a second set of textbooks to keep at home. The stress of not knowing what her homework was decreased when she used a homework app on her phone to keep track of assignments.

But there were some stressors on her list that that she couldn't easily change that were still very stressful for her. She worried so much about doing well in school that she sometimes couldn't do her homework. She felt stressed by having too much to do and not feeling like she could get everything done. She felt sad that she wasn't as popular as she would like to be. Her therapist taught her several ways to calm her mind and body. This really helped her feel better and improved her concentration so she could get things done. She also learned a few ways to focus her attention on the present moment instead of everything she was worried about, which decreased her stress level and helped her stay calm and present.

for you to do

Make a list of things that you find stressful in your life (your stressors). Be specific. (Examples: getting behind in homework, a poor grade in science, not having enough friends, conflict with parents about my messy room, fighting with my brother, not enough time to do everything)

_____

_____

_____

_____

_____

_____

_____

Use this list to identify the stressors you could do something to change or eliminate, and write down what you will do. (Examples: use a homework app, get a tutor, stop trying to be friends with someone who says hurtful things to you, take a study skills class, reduce your to-do list by one-third and stop trying to do so much, get extra time to take tests, ask your mom to keep your brother out of your room)

_____

_____

_____

_____

_____

_____

Think about ways to take care of yourself that help you de-stress and rejuvenate. (Examples: rest when you are tired, spend time outside in nature, get regular exercise, eat healthy foods, write in a journal, have some fun, meditate)

Write down what self-care is for you.

_____

_____

_____

_____

List three things that you can think of whenever you feel stressed to change the channel from your stress channel to your calm channel. (See activity 15.)

_____

_____

_____

… and more to do

Whenever you notice that you feel stressed out, use this instant de-stress process to relax and bring your attention to the present moment.

Set your intention to spend a moment turning down your stress level.

Take a slow breath in through your nose while you count to four.

Breathe out through your mouth while you count to eight.

Do it again. Inhale through your nose to the count of four and exhale through your mouth to the count of eight.

Now just breathe normally.

Bring your attention to your surroundings. Take a moment to notice what you see in front of you, beside you, above you, and below you.

Notice what you can hear around you.

Breathe in and pay attention to any fragrances or odors. Is the air warm, cool, or just right? Is it still or moving?

Now touch something with your fingers and notice the temperature, the texture, and everything there is to notice about how it feels.

Bring your attention to your body.

Tighten your hands and hold for seven seconds, then release them.

Smile and tighten your cheeks for seven seconds, then release them.

Bring your shoulders up to your ears and hold for seven seconds, then relax them.

Do a quick scan of your body and just notice how each part of your body feels, starting at your feet, moving up your legs to your hips, up to your stomach, your back, your shoulders, your arms and hands, your neck, your face, and your head.

If there is any tightness or discomfort in your body, take a deep breath in and fill that area with a cushion of healing and calming air. Let it go as you breathe out.

Bring your arms up over your head while you breathe in to the count of four.

71

Then exhale to the count of eight while you bring your arms down to your side.

Do this again three times.

Notice your current stress level.

Visit http://www.newharbinger.com/36255 to download an audio version of this meditation, and listen to it whenever you need to de-stress and focus on the present instead of worrying about the future or obsessing about what happened in the past.

noticing your surroundings and situation 17

for you to know

Having ADHD can sometimes make it difficult for you to be aware of yourself in your surroundings and situation. If you practice noticing your surroundings and situation with intention, you will be better able to center yourself and pay attention to the important things.

Jeremy often felt confused and out of it because he seemed to miss things that went on around him. When his therapist asked him what he would pay attention to in a classroom where the teacher was speaking, the classmate next to him was tapping his pencil, the lawnmower was going by the window, and the janitor walked by the classroom door, he said he would probably pay attention to the lawnmower or else try to pay attention to everything at once.

He often missed important information the teacher was explaining and didn't even realize it. Sometimes he didn't hear what chapter the teacher had asked the class to look at. Once he even raised his hand to answer a math problem from the wrong chapter. Everyone laughed. He was so embarrassed.

His therapist taught him a process he could use to notice his surroundings and his situation, to decide what he should be paying attention to, and to stay focused. With practice, he got better and better at knowing what he was supposed to be paying attention to in any given situation. And he soon noticed that he didn't seem to miss so much anymore.

for you to do

You can use the following process to notice your surroundings and decide what you need to pay attention to in any given situation.

- When you arrive in a new place, scan your surroundings and notice what is around you. What do you see, hear, and smell? What is going on around you?

- Bring your attention to the important thing(s).

- Decide what you need to pay attention to.

- Set your intention to pay attention to this.

- Focus on it.

- As soon as you notice you are paying attention to something else, simply bring your attention back to what you decided to pay attention to. Do this over and over.

Example 1: In the Classroom

When you first get to class, spend a moment just looking around the room. Decide what you need to pay attention to. Depending on what is going on in the class, this might be:

- a teacher who is speaking;

- the board, if a problem is written there for you to do or your assignment is listed there;

- your classmate who has raised a hand to answer or ask a question;

- your book or paper on your desk;

- the test on your desk; or

- your classmate if you are working in a group.

Once you have decided what to pay attention to, set your intention to focus on that. As soon as you notice you are distracted and thinking about something else, bring your attention back. Repeat this over and over again.

Example 2: With a Friend

When you are hanging out with a friend (and this could also be your boyfriend or girlfriend), think about what's important for you to pay attention to. This will include:

- what your friend is saying to you;

- the expression on your friend's face;

- your friend's body language;

- what your friend wants to do;

- opportunities to be kind and thoughtful, such as opening the door, helping with chores or homework, paying or sharing the bill for dinner, paying a compliment;

- asking about your friend's day or about something you know is important to him or her;

- showing interest in your friend's life; and

- finding things you have in common.

Think about what's *not* important to pay attention to:

- your cell phone

- everything that's going on around you

- yourself to the exclusion of your friend

- all the dialogue from your inner critic

- thoughts that are not about the present moment

... and more to do

With practice, you can improve your ability to pay attention to the important things around you.

List three surroundings and situations you spend time in, such as the classroom, with friends, on a date, at work, doing homework, and so on.

_____

_____

_____

For each of these, write down two important things to pay attention to. Put a star next to the one that is most important in each situation.

_____

_____

_____

_____

_____

_____

body surfing to calm and center yourself 18

for you to know

Teens with ADHD may feel stressed and anxious as they struggle to concentrate and do well in school, at their job, and with their friends. Taking a few minutes to do a body scan will help you relax, focus your mind, and tune in to what is going on in your body.

Jacob often felt stressed out and worried about everything he was trying to accomplish. His therapist taught him a body scan technique called body surfing to help him become more self-aware, relax, and improve his concentration. As he paid attention to his body one part at a time, he noticed that his mind quieted and that he felt more relaxed. He started body surfing for a few minutes at a time.

After he practiced daily for a couple of weeks, he realized that he could calm himself down more quickly and that it was easier to concentrate when he needed to. He noticed that it got easier to stay focused on his body, and he was able to increase the time until he could do so for fifteen minutes or more. He loved the way he felt after he finished scanning his whole body.

for you to do

Practice the following body surfing process to relax and de-stress, and to help you stop the busy clatter in your mind. Read through the script below and then when you understand the process, close your eyes and focus on each part of your body in turn as described in the script.

The purpose of this activity is to increase your awareness and notice any body sensations that may be present without trying to change them. If any uncomfortable feelings arise during the activity, you can stop at any time you need to. You are in complete control.

If you get distracted while doing this process, that's okay. As soon as you notice that you are not thinking about your body, just bring your attention back to the area of the body you were focusing on.

Find a quiet place where you won't be disturbed for a few minutes.

Find yourself a comfortable position, either lying flat on your back with arms and legs uncrossed or sitting in a chair with your feet flat on the floor and your hands resting gently on your lap or belly.

Breathe in slowly through your nose to the count of four: 1–2–3–4, and breathe out through your mouth even more slowly like you are blowing a huge bubble, to the count of 8: 1–2–3–4–5–6–7–8. Now just breathe normally.

Pause for a moment while you focus on your breath.

Imagine that a wave of attention is flowing over your entire body, starting at your feet.

Bring your attention to your left foot. Just notice everything there is to notice about your left foot, including your toes, heel, bottom of your foot, and top of your foot. Notice the skin, and the muscles inside. Notice what it feels like. Pay attention to whether there is any discomfort or tightness there. Is it cold, or hot? Does it feel light or heavy?

Continue to focus on your left foot for a few moments.

Then move the attention wave up to your left ankle. Notice how your left ankle feels. Imagine the muscles and tendons. Notice how it is flexible but strong at the same time.

Pause briefly while you focus on your left ankle.

Then pay attention to your left leg, starting at the bottom, moving up to your shins and calves, knees, and thighs, all the way to your hips at the top of your leg. Notice if your left leg feels tight or relaxed, warm or cold, light or heavy. What is the sensation there? Is it pleasant, unpleasant, or neutral?

Pause while you notice everything there is to notice about your left leg.

Now pay attention to your right foot. Just notice your right foot, including your toes, heel, bottom of your right foot, and top of your right foot. Notice what it feels like.

Stay focused on your right foot until you are ready to move on.

Then move up to your right ankle. Notice how your right ankle feels. Pay attention to whether there is any discomfort or tightness there. Is it cold or hot? Does it feel light or heavy?

Pause for a moment while you pay attention to your right ankle.

Then pay attention to your right leg, starting at the bottom, moving up to your shins and calves, knees, and thighs, all the way to your hips at the top of your leg. Notice if it feels tight or relaxed, warm or cold, light or heavy.

Continue to pay attention to your right leg for a few moments.

Now pay attention to both legs, from your toes up to your hips. Be still. Take a breath, and send your legs some kind and loving thoughts.

Stay focused on how your legs feel.

Now move your attention wave to your belly. Just notice what's there. Feel how your belly feels. Let it be the way it is. Send love and kindness to your belly.

Slow down and enjoy the feeling of love and kindness.

Now pay attention to your back, starting with your lower back all the way up to your shoulders. Notice how your back feels. Sit for a moment just noticing everything there is to notice about your back. What do you sense here? Notice how the muscles feel. Notice the strength of your back.

Keep paying attention to your back for a moment.

Now give your attention to your fingers, thumbs, and wrists, and on up your arms and shoulders. Just notice how your hands and arms feel.

Pause for a moment while you notice your arms.

Now pay attention to your neck and throat. Swallow, and notice how the muscles in your neck and throat feel.

Spend a moment noticing your neck and throat.

Now pay attention to your face: your chin, your mouth, your cheeks, your eyes, your eyebrows, your forehead, and finally your ears.

Pause here a moment.

Now bring your attention to your head, including your hair and scalp and your brain inside your head.

Stay focused on your brain for a moment.

Now that you have surfed the body attention wave all the way from your feet up to your head, take a big belly breath and fill your whole body with a cushion of air. Blow the air out gently like you are blowing a huge bubble, and let go of anything that needs to go.

Pause for a moment to notice what it feels like to let it go.

Open your eyes and bring your attention back to the room.

Take a moment to focus on your surroundings.

Notice how you feel now.

You can use the process of body surfing whenever you need it throughout the day. You can also use it periodically to push the reset button to lower your stress level and to train yourself to pay attention more easily.

Visit http://www.newharbinger.com/36255 to download an audio version of this meditation, and listen to it several times a week and whenever you need to calm down your mind and body and improve your ability to concentrate.

... and more to do

How can you make body surfing part of your day?

_____

_____

When would be a good time to use it?

_____

_____

How can you create a quick version of this body scan that you can use anytime, anywhere?

_____

_____

What do you like about doing this practice?

_____

_____

What do you think might get in your way of doing it regularly?

_____

_____

What can you do to address what might get in your way?

_____

_____

How do you think this body surfing practice will help you?

_____

_____

19 a core mindfulness practice

for you to know

Brain research shows us that our brains have the ability to change. This ability is called neuroplasticity. You can change your brain's ability to pay attention by practicing various mindfulness skills. These skills can be used throughout the day to bring your attention back to what you need to concentrate on—over and over again. It will get easier to concentrate with practice.

Alexis often struggled to concentrate and wished there was some way to improve her ability to pay attention. Her therapist explained that with practice Alexis could gradually teach her brain to concentrate more easily. Alexis was skeptical at first, but she had so much trouble concentrating that she was willing to try anything at this point.

She learned and practiced the core mindfulness practice her therapist taught her. At first, she noticed that she was distracted a lot and worried that it wouldn't work for her. Her therapist reassured her that as she practiced bringing her attention back each time she noticed it was off task she would be building and strengthening neuronal pathways in her brain that would gradually make it easier to concentrate. She stuck with it and discovered that she was distracted less often and that it was easier to bring her attention back when she was distracted.

She soon noticed that she was getting her math homework done more quickly than usual and that she could read her homework chapters longer before becoming distracted. She also noticed that she felt calmer and more present in her life. And when she practiced mindfulness when she was angry or upset, she felt like she had pushed the "reset" button to calm down and feel better quickly.

for you to do

Practice the following core mindfulness technique several times a day. Every time you notice that your mind has wandered and you are no longer thinking about your breath, remind yourself that it's normal for thoughts to wander. Just bring your attention back to your breath over and over again. It will get easier with practice, just like learning to walk or ride a bicycle got easier with practice. Start by doing this practice for thirty seconds. Set a timer on your phone or watch, and just keep focusing on your breath until you hear the alarm on the timer. When you can do this for thirty seconds, increase the time to one minute. When you have mastered one minute, try longer times up to ten or fifteen minutes.

Stop what you are doing for a few moments.

Close your eyes.

Be still.

Pay attention to your breathing.

Breathe slowly in through your nose and out through your mouth.

Imagine the air slowly filling your lungs and belly and then flowing out again.

If you notice that you are thinking about other things instead of your breath, that's okay. Just accept it, and then bring your attention back to your breath.

Notice your belly moving as you take slow belly breaths.

Listen to the sound of your breath.

Notice how your breath feels as it comes into you and goes back out.

Keep paying attention to your breath.

Notice how quickly or slowly you are breathing. Are your breaths deep or shallow?

When your mind wanders, just bring your attention back to your breath.

Continue for at least thirty seconds and lengthen this time as you are able until you can do this for fifteen minutes.

At the end of that time open your eyes and return to the room.

Visit http://www.newharbinger.com/36255 to download an audio version of this meditation.

... and more to do

Answer the following prompts after the first time you do the core mindfulness practice and then periodically to see how you are progressing.

How did you feel as you breathed?

_____

_____

_____

How often did your mind wander?

_____

What distracted you?

_____

_____

_____

How did you bring your attention back to your breath?

_____

_____

_____

What did you notice about your breath?

_____

_____

_____

Did your breathing change while you paid attention to it and if so, how?

_____

How long were you able to do this activity?

_____

When will you practice this every day? Schedule it on your calendar.

_____

How will you know when you are ready to increase the length?

_____

_____

What have you noticed about your ability to concentrate?

_____

_____

_____

Have you noticed any other changes in your life? (Examples: less worry, more focused, less angry, feeling better about yourself)

_____

_____

_____

20 how does your behavior impact others?

for you to know

Some teens with ADHD don't understand why other people avoid or dislike them. They might not realize how often they butt into conversations, how loud they talk, or how many times they say things impulsively that offend other people. You can tune into the behaviors you do that may be annoying to others so that you can reduce them and get along with people more easily.

Ethan wished he had more friends. Every time he thought he was making a new friend, something would happen and that person wouldn't want to be around him anymore. Some of his classmates even made fun of him and said nasty things about him.

Ethan felt sad and confused about why people didn't like him. His therapist asked him if he thought there was anything he was doing that put people off. With her help, Ethan made a list of things that might get in the way of attracting friends. Once he knew what behaviors he did that might be annoying others, he was able to be mindful of behaving in more appropriate ways.

He became aware that his extreme hyperactivity and constant talking were really annoying to his classmates. He practiced a meditation that enabled him to tune in to his body and quickly calm it down. He made a rule not to talk before stopping to think about why he was talking and whether it might be annoying others. When he found out that his mother thought he didn't care about her when he refused to clean his room because it didn't matter to him if it was clean, he chose to keep it cleaner to let her know she was important to him. He also learned and practiced better social skills in a social-skills group and slowly began making some friends.

for you to do

Below is a list of behaviors that teens with ADHD may engage in that could get in the way of friendships. Check off any that apply to you. Since you may not be aware of these behaviors, be sure to ask for input from family, friends, and teachers. Don't be offended if you don't like what they tell you. Remember, you are gathering information that will help you stop your behaviors that may be annoying to others or making it difficult to make friends.

☐ Talking too much

☐ Butting into conversations

☐ Interrupting

☐ Being bossy

☐ Saying things impulsively that hurt or offend others

☐ Making impulsive choices without considering the consequences to others

☐ Hyperactivity to the degree that it annoys others

☐ Not respecting personal space and getting too close to people physically

☐ Not listening

☐ Not paying attention to the other person

☐ Making poor choices due to impulsivity

☐ Missing or misinterpreting nonverbal cues

☐ Being loud

☐ Having trouble handling emotions

☐ Getting frustrated too easily

☐ Putting yourself down

☐ Acting angry and/or aggressive

☐ Not making eye contact

☐ Focusing too much on yourself

☐ Not showing interest in the other person

☐ Not realizing how your behavior makes other people feel

☐ Not finding anything in common with the other person

☐ Forgetting to do what you promised

☐ Arriving late

☐ Other _____

☐ Other _____

... and more to do

Pick two behaviors that you checked off above, and write down what you can change about each behavior that will be less annoying to others and work better for you to have friendships. Ask your therapist or parent for help with this if needed.

Behavior 1: _____

_____

Behavior 2: _____

_____

Practice changing these two behaviors for a week.

After you have changed each of these behaviors, write down what you did and how it worked out.

Behavior 1: _____

_____

Behavior 2: _____

_____

What other changes can you make?

Behavior 1: _____

_____

Behavior 2: _____

_____

21 taming your inner critic

for you to know

ADHD can sometimes make you feel bad about yourself. Even when you try so hard to do everything right, you may sometimes get distracted, forget to do things, and not get things done on time. Then your inner critic takes over and provides a running dialogue of criticism. You can feel better when you learn to tame your inner critic.

Emily often felt like she wasn't good enough and feared she would not be successful. When her therapist encouraged her to be mindful of what her inner voice was telling her, she noticed that it was often critical and judgmental and was usually putting her down. When she tuned in, she heard a running commentary that was critical about who she was and what she was doing. The voice said things like Forget it, you can't do that, don't even try *or* No one will ever go to the prom with you *or* You're a loser. *These negative statements made her feel incompetent, inadequate, inferior, guilty, ashamed, and afraid.*

Once she became aware of her inner critic, she used a process her therapist taught her to talk back to it, to acknowledge its efforts to keep her safe, and then to rewrite its critical and judgmental statements. She felt a profound feeling of relief when she noticed that the frequency of her inner critic's unhelpful comments decreased and she could transform the rest of them into statements that felt better.

for you to do

Answer the following questions to help you be more aware of what your inner voice says to you and how you feel when it is critical of you.

Step 1: Write down an example of when your inner voice was critical of you. (Examples: lost homework, got a lower grade than desired, while studying for a test, before auditioning for the play)

_____

_____

_____

Step 2: Write down what your inner critic said to you.

(Examples: *You are stupid; you will never get into college; you won't finish the test on time; you won't get the part.*)

_____

_____

_____

Step 3: Explain how you felt when your inner critic judged you or put you down.

(Examples: angry, not good enough, afraid, inferior)

_____

_____

Step 4: Write about how you would rather feel.

(Examples: confident, good enough, courageous, as good as)

_____

_____

Step 5: Write a more positive self-statement that feels better.

(Examples: "I sometimes lose things, but I am getting better at organizing my stuff"; "I wanted a better grade so next time I will study more"; "I will calm my test anxiety and get done on time"; "I will do my best.")

_____

_____

_____

Repeat Steps 1–5 for two other times when your inner voice was critical of you.

Step 1: _____

_____

_____

Step 2: _____

_____

_____

Step 3: _____

_____

_____

Step 4: _____

_____

_____

Step 5: _____

_____

_____

Step 1: _____

_____

_____

Step 2: _____

_____

_____

Step 3: _____

_____

_____

Step 4: _____

_____

_____

Step 5: _____

_____

_____

Practice noticing what your inner critic tells you and creating a more positive statement each time.

... and more to do

Use the following process to tame the inner critic by having a conversation with it that transforms its critical or judgmental statements into more positive and helpful self-statements.

1. Sit quietly for a moment.

2. Take a deep breath in through your nose and out through your mouth.

3. Tune in to what's going on inside you.

4. Notice what your inner voice says to you. Is what it says to you kind enough that you would you say it to a friend? Is it an inner critic? Does it judge you, put you down, tell you that you are not good enough, wrong, or guilty, or that you can't do something?

5. If it is an inner critic:

    *   Acknowledge it. Say to your inner voice, *I see you are judging me, inner critic. Thanks for your help. I know you are probably trying to keep me safe, help me be good, or help me be successful, but I don't need your help right now. Just because you judge me or criticize me doesn't mean that what you say is true.*

    *   Repeat aloud what the inner critic said to you; for example, *You are stupid* or *you will never get done in time.*

    *   Notice how you feel and how critical or judgmental the words sound.

    *   Replace the word "you" with "I," and rewrite what the critic said into a kinder self-statement; for example, "Even though I feel stupid sometimes, I'm actually pretty smart about some things" or "Although I have been late in the past, today I set my alarm to remind me to stay focused." Make sure your new self-statement is better but believable.

    *   Notice how you feel with the kinder, more positive statement.

    *   Notice how relieved you feel now that you have transformed the inner critic's negative or critical statements into statements that feel better and that you can believe.

Practice this process whenever you notice your inner critic is being critical or judgmental.

what do you like about yourself?

for you to know

Teens with ADHD often feel bad about themselves and focus primarily on the negatives. It is important to remember that everyone has strengths and positive qualities. Focusing on the things you like about yourself will help you feel better about yourself and increase your self-confidence.

Austin often didn't like himself very much because he couldn't get everything done on time and he sometimes felt like a failure. He often said things like, "I'm stupid"; "I hate myself"; "I wish I wasn't so bad at everything."

His therapist helped him explore how he often focused on the negative things about himself or his life. Then he helped Austin figure out what he did like about himself. When Austin learned how to focus on these things, he discovered that there were many things he really liked about himself. He realized that he was very helpful to his disabled grandmother, and that made him feel good. He loved his sense of humor and how his classmates responded when he told jokes. He loved the steady flow of creative ideas he always had. He remembered he got a good grade after he studied really hard for a test he had been worried about. He was really good in sports. He could quickly and correctly complete his math even if he didn't show his work. He noticed that he felt better when he chose to think about these things.

for you to do

To help you get in touch with things you like about yourself, write down three responses for each of the following:

Things you like about someone you know

1. _____
2. _____
3. _____

Things you enjoy doing

1. _____
2. _____
3. _____

Things you do well

1. _____
2. _____
3. _____

Things your parents like about you

1. _____
2. _____
3. _____

Things your friends, classmates, or siblings like about you

1. _____
2. _____
3. _____

Things your favorite teacher said about you

   1. _____

   2. _____

   3. _____

Your positive qualities

   1. _____

   2. _____

   3. _____

Things you like about your face

   1. _____

   2. _____

   3. _____

Things you like about your body

   1. _____

   2. _____

   3. _____

Things you like about your personality

   1. _____

   2. _____

   3. _____

activity 22 ✳ what do you like about yourself?

Things you like about helping someone else

1. _____
2. _____
3. _____

Things you've learned to do

1. _____
2. _____
3. _____

Kind things you said to someone else

1. _____
2. _____
3. _____

Kind things you did

1. _____
2. _____
3. _____

Things you believe in

1. _____
2. _____
3. _____

Personal strengths

    1. _____

    2. _____

    3. _____

Things you are proud of

    1. _____

    2. _____

    3. _____

Things you are glad you did

    1. _____

    2. _____

    3. _____

Review what you wrote above, and write down the three top things you like about yourself.

    1. _____

    2. _____

    3. _____

... and more to do

Practice the following meditation to help you identify, explore, and focus on the qualities, strengths, or skills you have that you like about yourself. Whenever you realize you are thinking about something you don't like about yourself, you can use this process to shift gears.

Find a quiet place where you won't be disturbed.

Sit quietly and close your eyes.

Take a deep breath in through your nose and let it out through your mouth.

Go gently within and notice how you feel.

Sometimes it can be hard to notice the good things about ourselves.

Everyone has different positive qualities, strengths, or skills.

Think about something you like about yourself.

It could be your smile, or how you play with your little brother.

Maybe you like how hard you try to do well.

Perhaps you like how kind you are to a neighbor.

Do you like how much energy you have?

Do you like being creative?

Do you like having lots of ideas?

Are you good at thinking outside the box?

Maybe you know how to really have fun.

Perhaps you like being mindful and present in your life.

Do you like your dreams for your future?

Just pick one thing you like about yourself and stay focused on it for a moment.

(Pause)

If other thoughts arise about things you don't like about yourself, that's okay. Just dismiss them and replace them with a thought about something you do like about yourself.

(Pause)

How do you feel while you think about something you like about yourself?

How does your body feel?

Would you rather think about things you like about yourself?

Visit http://www.newharbinger.com/36255 to download an audio version of this meditation.

23 why do you feel irritable or conflicted around your parents?

for you to know

Teens often have conflictual relationships with their parents. Teens with ADHD may have even more challenges getting along with parents due to their difficulty meeting parental expectations, completing chores, and regulating their emotions. Becoming mindful of the feelings triggered by interactions with your parents and what causes conflict will help improve your relationship and how you feel.

Tyler often felt irritable and angry with his parents. It seemed like they were always arguing with him, and he felt really bad when they yelled at him. He felt like they didn't understand him and like they were always on his case and telling him what to do. They never seemed to understand when he forgot to do his chores or didn't get his homework done. He wished they would let him do the things that all his friends could do. He wanted them to recognize his increasing maturity, his strengths, and his value. Sometimes he felt like they didn't really trust him. But sometimes he felt good about his parents and wanted to spend time with them. Although he often felt confused by his feelings, he knew he wanted their love and approval.

Tyler's therapist encouraged him to pay attention to how he felt during the next week each time he was interacting with his parents. Tyler did so and was surprised at how often he had conflicting feelings. On one hand, he loved his parents and knew they loved him. He wanted their encouragement and support and even welcomed some advice from time to time. On the other hand, he often felt angry, needed space, and desired more independence than they seemed willing to give him.

After Tyler identified his feelings, he then explored the source of his feelings. Often they were due to conflict with his parents. Sometimes they stemmed from his own inner conflict. He noticed that he sometimes felt like he could never please his parents, especially when his ADHD symptoms got in the way of getting things done. As he paid more attention to his feelings and got better at identifying their source, he noticed he had more control over his emotions and felt better about his relationship with his parents.

for you to do

Think about your interactions with your parents. How do you feel around them? Check all that apply and use the blank lines to add others.

☐ Loving

☐ Loved

☐ Validated

☐ Known

☐ Encouraged

☐ Valued

☐ Respected

☐ Understood

☐ Supported

☐ Trusted

☐ Admired

☐ Proud

☐ Confident

☐ Independent

☐ Happy

☐ Accepted

☐ Important

☐ Smart

☐ Okay

☐ Content

☐ Safe

☐ Calm

☐ Other: _____

☐ Other: _____

☐ Worried   ☐ Upset

☐ Resentful   ☐ Dependent

☐ Irritable   ☐ Judged

☐ Nervous   ☐ Rejected

☐ Conflicted   ☐ Stupid

☐ Angry   ☐ Not okay

☐ Dismissed   ☐ Unknown

☐ Annoyed   ☐ Nervous

☐ Misunderstood   ☐ Afraid

☐ Put down   ☐ Restricted

☐ Ignored   ☐ Oppressed

☐ Distrusted   ☐ Other: _____

☐ Confused   ☐ Other: _____

What causes conflict between you and your parents? Check all that apply, and use the blank lines to add others.

☐ Different opinions

☐ Misunderstanding each other

☐ Poor communication

☐ Jumping to conclusions

☐ Wanting more independence

☐ Lack of respect for my privacy

☐ Treating me like a child

☐ Trying or failing to meet their expectations

☐ Forgetting to do my chores

☐ Making poor or impulsive choices

☐ School

☐ Homework

☐ Grades

☐ ADHD symptoms

☐ Doing something they forbid me to do

☐ Wanting to do something they won't allow

☐ They don't like my friends

☐ What I wear

☐ How I wear my hair

☐ What I eat

☐ Where I go

☐ When I sleep

☐ Using their car

☐ A job

☐ Money

☐ After-school activities

☐ Siblings

☐ Parents' divorce

☐ College

☐ Other: _____

☐ Other: _____

☐ Other: _____

... and more to do

Answer the following questions to help you explore how to feel better around your parents.

List three ways your ADHD symptoms impact your relationship with your parents.

_____

_____

_____

_____

_____

Write down how you would like to feel around your parents.

_____

_____

_____

_____

_____

Describe what you can do differently to feel better around your parents. Be specific.

_____

_____

_____

_____

_____

How do you wish your parents would treat you differently than they do?

_____

_____

_____

_____

_____

How can you ask your parents for what you need?

_____

_____

_____

_____

_____

24 becoming responsible and independent

for you to know

Teens naturally yearn for independence from their parents. Your parents may feel that your ADHD symptoms impact your ability to show them you are responsible enough to gain the independence you desire. Becoming mindful of how your ADHD may interfere with this can help you make the changes needed to gain more independence.

Michael wished he could do what he wanted to do and go where he pleased without always having his parents on his case. He was sixteen, after all. And his friends were allowed to do things his parents simply refused to let him do. Sometimes he felt like his parents treated him like a baby and didn't let him make his own decisions. He hated it when they told him he wasn't responsible enough to do things he wanted to do. He just didn't understand why they wouldn't let him be more independent.

To help Michael clarify what he wanted, his therapist asked him some questions about responsibility and independence. Then he helped Michael explore how his ADHD might affect his ability to show he was responsible. Michael realized that he had a tendency to forget to do what his parents asked, or to forget to be home on time, and that he needed lots of reminding to get his homework done.

Michael began to understand why his parents might not feel he was ready for the independence he craved. With his new insight, he talked with his parents about what they needed him to do differently to prove that he was responsible enough to handle more freedom. He was delighted when his parents allowed him to use their car and hang out with his friends after he took their suggestion to use his calendar app and the alarm on his phone, which reminded him to let his parents know where he was and make sure he was home on time.

for you to do

Answer the following question to explore your desire for more independence.

How do you depend on your parents?

_____

_____

_____

_____

_____

In what areas do you want more independence?

_____

_____

_____

_____

_____

How do you think your ADHD prevents you from earning independence?

_____

_____

_____

_____

_____

activity 24 ✳ becoming responsible and independent

What is responsibility?

_____

_____

_____

_____

_____

What do you do that shows your parents you are responsible?

_____

_____

_____

_____

_____

How does your ADHD interfere with being responsible?

_____

_____

_____

_____

_____

How does your ADHD foster responsibility?

_____

_____

_____

_____

_____

What do you need to do differently to earn independence?

_____

_____

_____

_____

How can you ask your parents what you need to do differently to gain more independence?

_____

_____

_____

_____

… and more to do

List what you will do differently daily to earn the independence you desire. Post this list in your room where you can see it every day.

1. _____

2. _____

3. _____

4. _____

5. _____

6. _____

7. _____

8. _____

9. _____

10. _____

what does a healthy relationship look like? 25

for you to know

One important thing teens need to do is to develop healthy relationships both with their peers and adults. Teens with ADHD often struggle with this task. Maybe you are awkward in social situations, or maybe you say or do things that keep you from making strong connections to others. Becoming mindful of what constitutes a healthy relationship can help you create better relationships.

Jose often felt stressed out and lonely because he had trouble interacting with other people. He wondered if he was missing something because most of his classmates seemed to have friends, and many seemed to get along better than he did even with teachers. He worried that he didn't really know much about relationships or how to become more connected to others.

Jose's therapist encouraged him to explore the basics of a healthy relationship. He started by reviewing the great things that healthy relationships could do for Jose. Then he explained that relationships are about how two people are connected and that the features of a healthy relationship go both ways, meaning that what Jose gets from a healthy relationship is also what he needs to give to it.

Jose made a list of all the people in his life that he had a relationship with, such as his parents, siblings, classmates, teammates, and teachers. Next he wrote down what he got or would like to get from each relationship. Then he listed what he gave or could give to each relationship. Finally he considered his current relationships and what he could do to improve them.

for you to do

If you struggle to have healthy relationships, take time to understand what a healthy relationship looks like and how it feels. Explore the give-and-take that needs to occur to have a good connection with others. A healthy relationship has these six features:

1.   It makes you feel like you belong and are valued and connected.

2.   It improves your confidence and how you feel about yourself.

3.   It provides understanding, respect, trust, care, and safety.

4.   It provides a safe place to be and to learn about yourself.

5.   It encourages you to try out new ideas or discuss your opinions.

6.   It allows for sharing and developing common interests.

Make a list of at least ten people in your life you have a relationship with. Visit http://www.newharbinger.com/36255 to download a copy of this chart. Be sure to include family, friends, classmates, teachers, and others. Using the numbers that correspond to the features of a healthy relationship, fill in the remaining four columns. The first line has been completed as an example.

Name or relationship	What I get	What I would like	What I give	What needs work
John (classmate)	1	4, 6	1, 3, 6	4

After you complete this part of the activity, look over your chart and answer these questions:

Who do you enjoy being around?

_____

_____

_____

With whom do you like yourself most?

_____

_____

_____

Which relationships will you work to improve?

_____

_____

_____

Are there any relationships that should end? If so, which ones?

_____

_____

_____

Describe any patterns of what is missing from or present in your relationships.

_____

_____

_____

... and more to do

Think about your relationships and how they make you feel. Explore how your ADHD impacts them.

Write down what you think makes a good relationship.

_____

_____

_____

Describe what you like about one of your relationships.

_____

_____

_____

How do you choose your relationships and why?

_____

_____

_____

What can you do to improve a relationship that is not healthy?

_____

_____

_____

What gets in your way of having a healthy relationship?

_____

_____

_____

How does ADHD help your relationships? Be specific.

_____

_____

_____

How does ADHD impair your relationships? Be specific.

_____

_____

_____

What can you do differently to improve a specific relationship?

_____

_____

_____

Do you have a relationship that needs to end and if so, why?

_____

_____

_____

Think of a person you know. Close your eyes, and ask yourself the following questions while you remember spending time together.

- How do you feel when you are with this person?
- What happens in the relationship for you to feel that way?
- What messages do you get about yourself when you are with this person?
- What do you give to this relationship?
- What do you get from this relationship?
- Do your ADHD symptoms impact this relationship?
- Does this person accept you just as you are?

what makes a good friend? 26

for you to know

An important part of adolescence is developing friendships. Teens with ADHD often struggle to make and keep friends due to poor social skills, lack of self-awareness, and impulsive and hyperactive behavior that distances peers. You can learn and practice the skills needed to have friends.

Dylan wished he had more friends. He noticed that his classmates were often talking together or making plans for after school, and he felt left out or angry when they didn't include him. Every time he tried to talk with people in his class, they either ignored him or, even worse, made fun of him and said mean things. He was often accused of being too bossy, too intrusive, talking too much, interrupting, being loud, not listening, and not paying attention.

Dylan's classmate Preston also had ADHD, but unlike Dylan, Preston had many friends. Preston was outgoing and a lot of fun to hang out with. But Dylan noticed that sometimes Preston's friends became annoyed and impatient with Preston, too.

Dylan's therapist suggested that Dylan could learn skills he needed to make some friends. First, he helped Dylan explore what makes a good friend. Next, he encouraged Dylan to think about and be mindful about what he might be doing that interfered with developing friendships. And then, he guided Dylan on the use of some specific skills that helped him connect more successfully. Dylan soon had a friend to sit with at lunch and someone to hang out with after school sometimes, and he felt much better.

for you to do

Think about the friendships you have or would like to have, and answer these questions:

What do you think makes a good friend?

_____

_____

_____

Name someone you are or would like to be friends with. _____

What do you like about this person?

_____

_____

_____

What does this person do that makes him or her a friend?

_____

_____

_____

_____

What do you do that makes you a friend?

_____

_____

_____

_____

How has ADHD interfered with your friendships? Give specific examples. (Examples: I interrupted Sally, and she was annoyed with me; I had trouble sitting still while talking to John; I talk all the time and didn't notice that Devin wanted to talk until he got mad and walked away; I never make eye contact and didn't notice that Casey wasn't interested in what I was saying; I don't know how to connect with people; I forgot what Mom told me to do because I wasn't paying attention when she told me; I lost my brother's jacket; I got really angry and lost my cool when David ignored me today.)

_____

_____

_____

_____

_____

_____

_____

_____

_____

... and more to do

Post the following list of affirmations containing important social skills where you can see it, and read them out loud once per day for a week. Find a time when you can read these statements each day; for example, before you get out of bed, while you brush your teeth, when you get home from school, after dinner, or before you turn off the light to sleep. As you read them, think of a time when you did or will do each one.

After the first week, read them out loud at least once a week. Remind yourself to actually do them when you are with people, and practice them until they become automatic. For example, smile at every person you see. Notice what happens as well as how you feel when you actually do them.

I will say hello.

> **What to do:** Greet people by saying hello or hi.
>
> **How this helps:** This will show that you noticed them and that you are friendly.

I will smile.

> **What to do:** Smile when you say hello.
>
> **How this helps:** This will let people know you are happy to see them. They will feel good.

I will make eye contact when I interact with people.

> **What to do:** When you are talking to others, look at their eyes long enough to notice what color they are. Don't stare, but make eye contact enough that they know you are listening and interested in what they have to say.
>
> **How this helps:** Doing this will help you connect and show people you are paying attention to them.

I will listen.

> **What to do:** Listen well enough to ask them questions about what they said or make kind comments about it.
>
> **How this helps:** This will help you learn about others and show them you are interested in them and understand what they said.

I will let people finish without interrupting.

> **What to do:** Even if you are bursting to say something, practice waiting for your turn to speak. No one likes to be interrupted.
>
> **How this helps:** Waiting for them to finish will let them know you are interested in hearing what they are saying and that you care.

I will show interest in people.

> **What to do:** Ask questions like, "How long have you lived here?" or "What kind of music do you enjoy?" or "How do you like that math class?"
>
> **How this helps:** This is a great way to find something in common and make a connection.

I will let them know I understand.

> **What to do:** Say things like, "Yeah, I know how you feel. I was really upset when that happened to me"; "Wow! That must have been tough to fail the driving test"; or "Gee, I'm sorry to hear about your accident."
>
> **How this helps:** This will help others feel heard and validated. They will feel like you "get" them.

I will give them compliments.

> **What to do:** Say things like, "I like your hair"; "You did a great job on that report"; or "That's a cool shirt."
>
> **How this helps:** Compliments will make them feel good around you and make them want to spend more time with you.

I will share something about my life, including what is hard for me.

> **What to do:** Share information like, "I love to ski"; or "I have to work really hard in math"; or "Sometimes I just can't concentrate."
>
> **How this helps:** Sharing about your life will help others connect with you and find things in common with you. Sharing your struggles will help them see that you are real and approachable.

I will be helpful.

> **What to do:** For example, ask, "Can I get that door for you?" or "Can I help you carry that?"
>
> **How this helps:** This will show that you noticed them and that you are kind and caring.

I will be encouraging.

> **What to do:** Say things like, "Don't worry. You will do great on the test" or "Looks like you are really learning this math."

> **How this helps:** People like to be acknowledged and to have their efforts noticed and will want to be around you.

I will find things we have in common.

> **What to do:** For example, say, "I like to play guitar, watch movies, and play video games. What do you like to do?" or "I'm going for a walk. Do you like to walk?"

> **How this helps:** The things you have in common are like the glue that holds relationships together. If you don't have anything in common, you will soon drift apart.

I will represent myself using "I" statements.

> **What to do:** For example, say, "I enjoy talking with you. I would like to get together and get to know you better" or "I feel left out. I would love to be included next time."

> **How this helps:** Using "I" statements is a healthy and nonjudgmental way to represent yourself and share who you are and what you like with others.

I will be kind.

> **What to do:** Make statements like, "Would you like some help with your math?" or "Can I get you a soda?" or "I love the way you handled that."

> **How this helps:** Kindness is a central ingredient of being mindful and helps you connect with others and feel good about yourself while helping.

I will be more self-aware.

> **What to do:** For example, stop tapping your fingers as soon as you notice it so you don't annoy your classmate. Avoid hogging the conversation. Ask others what they would like to do, so you are not seen as bossy. Tune into your feelings so you can manage your emotions.

> **How this helps:** Being self-aware will help you be more present in relationships and behave in socially acceptable ways that help others feel comfortable around you.

I will spend time around people I would like to be like and that I feel good around.

> **What to do:** Focus on kind, honest, helpful people. Be mindful about how you feel around people, and choose those that bring out the best in you.

> **How this helps:** Spending time with people you feel good around will encourage you and boost your confidence and self-esteem. Also, you will tend to become more like those you spend time with.

I will make friends with people who accept me and embrace me for who I am.

> **What to do:** Choose healthy people who are accepting, kind, encouraging, understanding, and helpful. Limit your exposure to people who are critical, judgmental, rejecting, and mean.

> **How this helps:** This will help you feel good about yourself and you will be more likely to be happy and healthy.

Visit http://www.newharbinger.com/36255 to download a copy of these affirmations. Print them out and post them where you can see them and read them out loud daily. Notice how your friendships change as you use this practice and as you gradually start doing what you are reading.

27 why do you want to hang out with this person?

for you to know

Teens normally become interested in hanging out together and having romantic relationships. Although this can be challenging for teens with ADHD, you can be more successful by being mindful of your feelings and understanding what attracts you to a particular person as well as when a relationship should end. Being aware of how your ADHD symptoms impact your relationships will also improve your success.

Brittany really liked Kyle, a boy she sat next to in math class. She really wanted him to notice her and to like her. She thought about him all the time, even when she was supposed to be studying. Brittany wondered if it was normal to be so obsessed about a boy she hardly knew.

Brittany's therapist assured her that it is normal to notice boys and want to be noticed back. He asked her to think about how she felt when she was around Kyle and to write down why she liked him. Brittany noted that she felt excited, anxious, and then let down when Kyle ignored her. She felt embarrassed around him and often didn't know what to say. When she tried to talk with him, he seemed to ignore her and sometimes put her down when she didn't have her homework organized for class or if she forgot to raise her hand before speaking. She also felt uncertain of herself. She didn't know for sure why she liked him, except that he was handsome and smart and had a lot of friends. When Brittany's therapist asked her what she had in common with Kyle, she said that they were in the same math class but she couldn't think of anything else.

When her therapist asked her if there were other boys she interacted with, Brittany told him about Ethan, a boy in her science class who always smiled at her and asked her about her day, and often made her laugh. When she stopped to think about him, she realized that Ethan was good looking and kind, and loved the same bands she enjoyed. Plus he noticed her and enjoyed her impulsive humor and high energy. He even helped her with her homework when she had trouble organizing her papers. She felt comfortable, accepted, and sure of herself around Ethan.

Taking time to be mindful of how she felt around these two boys and noticing what they had in common with her helped Brittany see that she didn't really feel good about herself around Kyle. She realized she felt much better around Ethan and had more in common with him. She decided to pay more attention to getting to know Ethan.

for you to do

Spend a few moments thinking about someone you would like to or are already hanging out with or dating. Use the following process to explore the relationship, how it makes you feel, and how your ADHD impacts it.

Write down his or her name. _____

How do you feel about yourself when you are around this person?

_____

_____

_____

How does this person treat you?

_____

_____

_____

Does this person know you have ADHD? _____

Do your ADHD symptoms get in your way of connecting with this person and if so, how?

_____

_____

_____

Do your ADHD symptoms enhance this relationship and if so, how?

_____

_____

_____

How does this person react when you do something ADHD-related, like being distracted, not concentrating, being disorganized or late, being impulsive or hyperactive, or having high energy?

_____

_____

_____

Does this person see your strengths, abilities, and gifts and if so, which ones?

_____

_____

_____

Does this person accept you the way you are or want you to change and if so, how?

_____

_____

_____

... and more to do

Explore and evaluate a current relationship, with the goal of deciding whether it is a healthy relationship or one that needs to end.

List at least five things you have in common.

_____

_____

_____

Explain why this is a good person for you to spend time with.

_____

_____

_____

Explore your feelings, both good and bad, about this person.

_____

_____

_____

What, if anything, do you wish was different about this person?

_____

_____

_____

List red flags (warning signs) you notice about this relationship, if any.

_____

_____

_____

In what ways do you need to change for this relationship to work, if any?

_____

_____

_____

Which features of a healthy relationship does this relationship contain? (You can look back at activity 25 to refresh your memory of these features.)

_____

_____

_____

Which features of a healthy relationship does this relationship lack?

_____

_____

_____

Do you have similar intentions about sexual activity?

_____

_____

_____

Do your intentions align concerning drug and alcohol use?

_____

_____

_____

How are your values and beliefs similar or different?

_____

_____

_____

Why is this a relationship you think you should continue, or why is it time to move on?

_____

_____

_____

28 social skills for connecting and hanging out

for you to know

Connecting with someone special can be exciting and rewarding as well as challenging for teens with ADHD. Being mindful of essential social skills makes it easier to connect and to create a healthy relationship.

Andrew liked talking with Ashley and wanted to ask her to hang out. He didn't know what to say, and he worried that she would turn him down. He was feeling unsure of himself because he had hung out with a few girls before but none of them worked out very well for him. One girl told him that he didn't pay attention to her and always seemed distracted, which made her feel invisible. Another told him that he never asked her what she wanted to do. One told him he talked too much and didn't seem interested in her life. One was angry because he often arrived late. And another told him he was moving way too fast for her and was getting ahead of himself.

Andrew's ADHD coach thought Andrew needed help with some social skills. He noticed that Andrew rarely made eye contact when they spoke. He also saw that Andrew often tuned out and spent time looking at his phone during their conversations. He helped Andrew explore how his behavior might be making people feel like he wasn't interested in them.

His coach then helped Andrew with some skills he could use to connect with someone he wanted to hang out with. After Andrew practiced his coach's suggestions, he became more comfortable around girls he liked. He was able to show them he was interested in getting to know them and to find out what they had in common. Although not everyone said yes when he asked them to hang out, he felt more sure of himself and had fun connecting.

for you to do

Complete the following process to practice social skills until they become automatic and you feel comfortable doing them. Although this section uses "she" and "her," you can replace them with "he" and "him" as needed.

Practice making eye contact with people you are comfortable with, such as family members or friends. What color are their eyes? Are they looking at you or somewhere else? How did you feel making eye contact?

_____

_____

_____

Make eye contact with three people you don't know and say hi.

What happened when you did this? How did you feel?

_____

_____

_____

Think of someone you are interested in or already hanging out with.

Make eye contact and say hi to that person.

How did you feel when you did this?

_____

_____

_____

How did she respond?

_____

_____

_____

Introduce yourself if you don't know her. What did you say?

_____

_____

Do you think she is interested in talking to you and if so, what did she do that makes you think so?

_____

_____

_____

Comment on something you notice about her or about something immediately in your surroundings. (Examples: "I see we have the same science class"; "How did you do on the homework last night?"; "That blue is a great color on you"; "Wow, it sure is raining.")

Write down three things you can say.

_____

_____

_____

Show interest by asking her opinion about something or asking about what she likes to do. (Examples: "What did you think of the video we watched in class?" "Did you do anything fun over the weekend?")

Write down three ways you can show interest in her.

_____

_____

_____

Find things you have in common with each other. (Example: "What bands do you like?"; "Seen any good movies lately?"; "What do you like to do when you aren't in school?")

Write down three things you have in common.

_____

_____

_____

... and more to do

Here, you can mentally replace "he" and "him" with "she" and "her," if that works better for you. Practice asking someone to do something that you know he might enjoy. (Examples: "Some of us are heading to the beach after class. I know you love to swim. Want to go?"; "Hi, I enjoy talking with you. Would you be interested in going to see that movie you mentioned wanting to see?"; "Hi, I have two tickets to see your favorite team play this weekend. Want to go with me?")

Write down three things you can say to ask him to hang out.

_____

_____

_____

Ask him out or tell him you would like to hang out.

What did you say? What did he say? How did you feel?

_____

_____

_____

If he said no, why do you think he did so? Did he really have other plans? Was he not interested in going on a date with you?

_____

_____

_____

If he wasn't interested in hanging out with you, write down options for what to do next. (Examples: realize that this person isn't a good match and move on, keep interacting until you know each other better, try again)

_____

_____

_____

Describe a time when someone showed interest in you.

_____

_____

_____

How did you feel?

_____

_____

_____

If you were interested in this person, describe why, and if you weren't interested, explain why not.

_____

_____

_____

What can you say to show interest back?

_____

_____

_____

What can you say to be kind if you are not interested?

_____

_____

_____

When you are hanging out together

- arrive at least five minutes early;
- make frequent eye contact without staring;
- give him your full attention;
- put away your phone;
- listen to what he is saying well enough to ask a question or make a comment about it;
- discuss what you both want to do; and
- follow through on what you promised him that you would do.

Describe what went well when you were together.

_____

_____

_____

Describe what didn't go well when you were together.

_____

_____

_____

How did you feel while you were together?

_____

_____

_____

How did your ADHD symptoms impact your time together, if at all? Include both positive and negative impact.

_____

_____

_____

What can you do differently next time to make things go even better?

_____

_____

_____

Does he seem interested in moving forward with a relationship at the same rate you are? Describe how you can tell.

_____

_____

_____

List three things he said or did that indicated he enjoyed being with you.

_____

_____

_____

List three things he said or did that indicated he was not interested in you.

_____

_____

_____

Section 4

How to Live a Healthy Life

Teens with ADHD function better when they get enough sleep, eat well, and make beneficial decisions about the use of alcohol and drugs. This section will help you get the sleep you need to perform at your peak. It will also help you be mindful of what and when you eat and how you drive, and will help you explore options for making healthy choices about drugs and alcohol.

29 how much sleep do you need?

for you to know

Teens with ADHD often have difficulty getting enough sleep. You may stay up too late or have trouble falling asleep or getting up on time. ADHD symptoms tend to multiply in intensity when you are sleep deprived. Figuring out how much sleep you need to function at your peak can help you get the sleep you need and improve your daytime functioning.

Jared was exhausted all the time. He had trouble concentrating and often fell asleep in class. He wished he could have more energy. He knew he probably wasn't getting enough sleep, but he didn't really know how much was enough or how to improve his sleep pattern to get it. He often stayed up really late and had a lot of trouble getting up in the morning. He slept very late every chance he got, but even then he still felt tired. And sometimes he woke up really early and couldn't go back to sleep even though he was tired. Yuck!

Jared's therapist asked him to keep track of his sleep pattern for a week. To remind him to write down what time he went to bed, Jared placed a bright yellow sticky note where he would see it as he got into bed. In the morning he recorded when he thought he fell asleep, and when he woke up. Then he rated his daytime tiredness on a scale of 0–5 where 5 is the most tired. After a couple of nights, he decided to use the calendar app on his phone to keep track of these times instead of writing them down.

When Jared looked over his sleep pattern for a week, he noticed that when he didn't get at least six hours a night he was really exhausted the next day. He noticed that on those days his concentration was really poor, he couldn't process information well, and his mood was low. He realized that he felt best when he got about nine hours of sleep, which rarely happened. He figured out when he needed to go to bed in order to get nine hours of sleep and get up on time. He used an alarm to remind himself to go to bed in time each night. When he did this for a whole week, he felt like a new person. He had more energy, his concentration was better, and he felt less cranky and more enthusiastic about his life.

for you to do

Think about how you know you are tired. Do you fall asleep during the day, in class, while reading, or while riding in the car? Do you have extra trouble concentrating? Do you fidget and have more trouble sitting still? Are you cranky and grumpy, or easily annoyed and quickly frustrated? Do you have trouble motivating yourself to do things? These can all be signs of tiredness. List the signs that you are tired.

_____

_____

_____

Place a brightly colored sticky note where you will see it as you go to bed to remind you to write down when you went to bed. Use this sleep diary (or type the times into your calendar app) to track your current sleep pattern, and rate your daytime tiredness on a scale from 0 (no tiredness) to 5 (extremely tired). Set an alarm to remind yourself to fill this out every day for one week.

Day	Went to bed	Went to sleep (estimated)	Awoke the next morning	Total hours slept	Tiredness rating (0–5) the next day
Monday					
Tuesday					
Wednesday					
Thursday					
Friday					
Saturday					
Sunday					

Visit http://www.newharbinger.com/36255 to download a copy of the diary.

... and more to do

Use your completed sleep diary to figure out how much sleep you need.

What's the most sleep you got? _____

On a scale of 0 to 5 (where 5 is extremely tired), how tired were you when you slept this much?
_____

What's the least amount of sleep you got? _____

On a scale of 0 to 5, how tired were you when you slept this much?_____

How many hours of sleep per night make you feel the best? _____

Now figure out your ideal bedtime.

What time do you have to get up in the morning? _____

How many hours of sleep do you need to feel your best? _____

Subtract the number of hours of sleep you need from the time you have to get up. _____

Example:

If you need to get up at 6:30 a.m., and you need eight hours of sleep, then your ideal bedtime is 10:30: (6:30 a.m.—8 hours = 10:30 p.m.)

Keep in mind that most teens function better with nine hours.

for you to know

Teens with ADHD often don't get the sleep they need because they either stay up too late or have trouble falling asleep once they are in bed. Designing and following a bedtime routine can help you get the sleep you need to thrive.

Hailey often had trouble getting to bed in time to get enough sleep. Sometimes she put off doing her homework until she had to stay up really late to finish it. She often got distracted talking with friends, watching TV, or just chilling out. Occasionally she was so exhausted that she went right to sleep, but usually when she got into bed she had trouble quieting her mind enough to fall asleep.

Hailey's ADHD coach helped her figure out what time she needed to be in bed in order to get enough sleep to function well, and together they designed a bedtime routine for Hailey to follow each night. First, Hailey made a list of things she was typically doing during the evening. Then she eliminated some things and rescheduled some to do during the day so she would have time for the most important evening activities. Then she determined what time she needed to be in bed to feel her best and worked backward to create a routine that let her finish her nighttime activities and allow time to calm down her brain and get to sleep on time. Setting an alarm for when she should start her bedtime routine helped Hailey finish up what she was doing and focus on preparing for sleep.

At first, Hailey had trouble getting her homework done in time because she procrastinated and didn't get started soon enough. When she set an alarm to remind her to start her homework, she was able to finish in time. She sometimes had to adjust her schedule to accommodate an evening sport, a school event, or her part-time job. As she paid more attention to her bedtime routine, it got easier to get in bed at her ideal bedtime. When she listened to a sleep meditation that helped her relax, she could go to sleep more quickly.

After following her bedtime routine for two weeks, Hailey found it much easier to get everything done, to calm down her busy mind, to get to bed on time, and to fall asleep quickly. She realized that she felt much better and was more productive when she got enough sleep.

for you to do

Designing a sleep routine can help you get your activities done in time to get to bed at your ideal bedtime. Then you will be prepared to fall asleep faster, get the sleep you need, and function better the next day.

To figure out how much time you need to get your evening activities done, list the activities you need to do in the evening and how much time each activity takes.

Activity	Time Needed

Add up the total time needed: _____

What time do you need to go to bed? (You can check back to activity 29 for your ideal bedtime.)
_____

How much time is there to do all your nighttime activities before bedtime? _____

If there isn't enough time, what can you eliminate or move to another time of day?

_____

_____

_____

_____

You can fall asleep faster if you follow a routine that calms you and prepares your brain for sleep. Review the following checklist, fill in the times requested, and check off each item as you think about how you can incorporate them into your life.

☐ I will avoid sugary foods, caffeine, and artificial colors after four p.m.

☐ My ideal bedtime is: _____

☐ I will go to bed at the same time every night.

☐ If I take stimulant medications, I will talk to my prescriber about rescheduling the dose if it is not worn off by my ideal bedtime.

☐ In order to be in bed on time I must complete homework by: _____

☐ I must start my homework by: _____

☐ I will use an alarm that repeats every night to remind me to start my homework.

☐ I will stop exercise at least two hours before bedtime.

☐ I will avoid violent or overly stimulating TV shows two hours before bedtime.

☐ I will stop activities that activate my brain at least an hour before bedtime.

☐ I will stop texting and using social media an hour before bedtime.

☐ I will have a low sugar, caffeine-free snack an hour or more before bedtime.

☐ I will set an alarm that repeats every night to remind me when to get ready for bed.

☐ I will stop activities and calm my mind and body an hour before my ideal bedtime.

☐ I will shut off my computer, TV, tablet and/or phone an hour before bedtime.

☐ I will take a warm and relaxing bath.

☐ I will turn down the lights a half hour before bedtime.

☐ I will close the shades to keep my room dark while I am sleeping.

☐ I will turn off noise that might disturb my sleep and use a sound machine to mask noise if needed.

☐ I will make sure my bed is comfortable.

☐ I will wear comfortable sleeping clothes.

☐ I will listen to quiet music.

☐ I will read. (Books are preferable to avoid light activation. If you do choose to use your tablet, dim the brightness so the light doesn't make it harder to fall asleep.)

☐ I will listen to a sleep meditation to fall asleep.

... and more to do

Using the checklist above, design your own personal nighttime routine. Review it every night for at least two weeks to remind yourself to follow it until it becomes a habit that you do automatically every night. Once your routine is established, notice when you are starting to fall out of your routine, and review it again to get back on track. This will help you be ready for bed at the same time every night and get enough sleep to feel rested and alert every day.

Sample schedule for nighttime routine:

Time	Task or Activity
7:30–9:30	Homework. Eat a healthy snack while completing homework.
9:30	When alarm goes off, turn off TV, computer, phone. Spend five minutes putting things away in my room.
9:45	Get ready for bed.
10:00	Read, listen to music, listen to meditations for planning or relaxation.
10:15	Turn lights out and listen to sleep meditation.
10:30	Fall asleep.
6:30	Alarm goes off; wake up and get out of bed.

Fill in the schedule below to create your personalized nighttime routine, and post it where you can see it every night:

Time	Task or Activity

Visit http://www.newharbinger.com/36255 to download a copy of this form.

sleep meditation to calm your mind and body 31

for you to know

Teens rarely get the ideal amount of sleep that studies suggest they need. The busy mind so common to those with ADHD can make it difficult to get good enough sleep. Listening to a sleep meditation can help you calm and relax your mind and body so you can fall asleep faster.

Geordan had so much trouble falling asleep that she felt tired all the time. She was starting to dread going to bed because she couldn't quiet her mind and body enough to fall asleep. She hated lying in bed sometimes for hours before she finally fell asleep. She just couldn't shut off her busy mind. Then she felt exhausted the next day and had much more trouble staying focused than usual.

Geordan's therapist suggested that she listen to a sleep meditation that would help her relax her mind and body enough to fall asleep. Geordan was willing to try anything that might help, although she didn't understand how just listening to something could help her fall asleep. She downloaded a sleep meditation to her phone and listened to it after she got into bed and turned off the lights.

At first she had a little trouble staying focused on the recorded voice that was leading her into a relaxed place, but she realized that even the first time she used it she must have fallen asleep before the end because she didn't remember hearing the recording finish. She continued to listen to the sleep meditation nightly for a few weeks and gradually noticed that she wasn't feeling as tired anymore during the day. Hooray! Occasionally she was still awake when the meditation ended, so she would just start it over again, and she would still fall asleep sooner than before she had started using it.

for you to do

Use the sleep meditation below to relax your mind and body, let go of your day, and fall asleep.

Find a comfortable position to fall asleep. Bring your attention to your breath.

Take a deep breath in through your nose to the count of four. Then exhale slowly through your mouth to the count of eight, like you are blowing a large bubble.

Do it again. Inhale peace, calm, and relaxation. As you exhale, relax your mind.

Do it one more time. Inhale comfort, safety, and healing. As you exhale, relax your mind.

Focus on your toes and feet. Let any tension stored there flow down through the bottoms of your feet and onto the floor.

Bring your attention to your legs, starting with your ankles, shins and calves, knees, and thighs. Just notice what's there and allow anything that needs to go to flow down through your legs, your feet, and out through the bottoms of your feet.

Pay attention to your hips, bottom, and belly. Let any tightness flow down through your thighs, knees, calves and shins, and out through the bottoms of your feet.

Notice your back, from your lower back all the way to your shoulders. Again let anything that needs to go flow down through your bottom, your thighs, your knees, your calves and shins, and out through the bottoms of your feet.

Notice your stomach, chest, and heart area. Take a deep cleansing breath, and fill your lungs with a cushion of healing air. As you exhale, let go of anything that needs to go. You just don't need it. Remember a time when you felt thankful for something.

Notice your hands, fingers, thumbs, and wrists. Let go of anything you are holding on to, and let it flow out through the ends of your fingers.

Concentrate on your shoulders and neck, and let anything stored here flow down through your arms, your wrists, your hands, and right out through the ends of your fingers and onto the floor.

Pay attention to your face, including your jaw, cheeks, eyes, and forehead. Scrunch up your cheeks and eyes; hold for a moment and then release.

Focus on your scalp. Allow anything that needs to go to flow down your neck to your shoulders and down your arms to your wrists and hands and out through the ends of your fingers onto the floor.

Pay attention to your brain. Imagine you are inside your head, turning the controls to slow things down. Watch as your brain calms and rests, slowly lets go of your day, and falls asleep.

Know that you will sleep deeply throughout the night and wake up exactly at the right time, feeling rested, rejuvenated, and focused.

Take a deep cleansing breath and fill your entire body with a cushion of calming energy. As you exhale, allow yourself to go deeper into restful sleep.

Enjoy the feeling of deep relaxation and calm, restful sleep.

Good night.

Visit http://www.newharbinger.com/36255 to download an audio version of this meditation.

... and more to do

Take a few moments to reflect on what happened when you listened to the sleep meditation.

What was it like trying to pay attention to the words?

_____

_____

_____

If you got distracted, how did you bring your attention back to the meditation?

_____

_____

_____

What did you think about, and were you able to calm your mind?

_____

_____

_____

What did your body feel like?

_____

_____

What was it like to notice your mind and body?

_____

_____

What was it like to let go and relax?

_____

_____

_____

How did listening to this meditation impact your ability to fall asleep?

_____

_____

_____

How did your sleep change or stay the same after listening to this meditation?

_____

_____

What did you notice the next day about your energy level?

_____

_____

_____

Were you aware of any changes in your ability to concentrate the next day?

_____

_____

_____

What do you like least about listening to the meditation?

_____

_____

_____

What do you like most about how you feel when you listen to the meditation?

_____

_____

_____

32 paying attention when you are eating

for you to know

Teens need a healthy diet to support their still-developing brains and bodies. Those with ADHD often have specific nutritional deficiencies that need to be addressed. When you are mindful about making food choices that support your brain's health, as well as being fully present when you eat, you will ensure that your diet is nutritious and healthy.

Madison didn't pay much attention to what she ate every day. She tended to eat a lot of fast food and sugary treats. She didn't think it mattered much. But she was often exhausted by midafternoon and then had even more trouble concentrating and motivating herself than usual.

Madison's ADHD coach asked her keep a food diary where she would write down everything she ate or drank for four days. When they reviewed her food diary, her coach pointed out that Madison wasn't eating enough protein, fruits, vegetables, and water, and often went way too long between meals or snacks. One day she had no breakfast and then only milk and potato chips for lunch! He explained that her brain needed high-quality fuel every few hours to function at its peak, just like a car needed gas. Her eating habits meant she was running on empty much of the time.

He recommended that she limit sugar and caffeine, as these activated the brain, which felt good, but then later left her feeling exhausted, with no energy. He suggested she ask her doctor to test her zinc, magnesium, iron, and omega-3 levels, which are often deficient in those with ADHD.

Then he taught her a mindful eating process to help her slow down and be fully present each time she ate. This helped her to pay attention to what she ate, to enjoy it more, and to make food choices that served her better.

for you to do

Completing a food and symptom diary can help you become aware of what you eat and whether what you eat makes your ADHD symptoms better or worse.

Using the example in the diary that follows, write down everything you eat or drink for four days. Include when you ate it, and then rate your energy, focus, hyperactivity, and mood on a scale of 0–10, where ten is the worst.

After you do this for four days, review your diary to notice your food choices and patterns for when and what you eat. Pay attention to how your symptoms change after you eat certain foods. Use this information to mindfully choose foods that support your brain health and decrease your ADHD symptoms. Visit http://www.newharbinger.com/36255 to download a copy of this diary, and print out enough pages for four days.

Food and Symptom Diary

Time	Food and drink	Symptom Rating (0–10)			
		Energy	Focus	Hyperactivity	Mood
7:00 a.m.	Milk, eggs, toast	2	3	3	5

... and more to do

When you eat mindfully you bring your attention to the present moment, notice and enjoy what you eat, are more aware of when you are full, and make better food choices. Practice this process in your imagination, and then use it for a few minutes each time you eat.

Close your eyes and pretend that you are eating.

Set your intention to pay attention to everything there is to notice about eating.

Whenever thoughts arise that are not about eating, notice them, dismiss them, and remind yourself of your intention to pay attention to eating.

Imagine you are looking at your favorite food. What food is it? Notice how the food looks as it sits on your plate. Be aware of the food's smell, color, and shape.

Spend a moment thinking about where this food came from and all the things that had to happen for it to be here in this moment for you to eat.

Before you start to eat, pay attention to how your stomach feels. Does it feel full or empty? Is it comfortable or uncomfortable? Can you connect how it feels with hunger? Make sure you are hungry before you eat.

As you put food on your fork, notice how it feels in your hand. Is it heavy or light?

Take a sniff and notice what the food smells like.

As you place the food in your mouth, notice if it is warm or cold. How does it feel in your mouth, on your tongue, and on your teeth?

Pay attention to how it feels when you chew the food. Focus on the flavor and the texture. Is it crunchy, chewy, soft, or hard? Notice if it is tender, tough, slippery, smooth, rough, salty, tangy, sweet, sour, spicy, or plain. Be aware of whether it sticks to your teeth.

If your mind wanders, that's okay. Just remember your intention and bring your attention back to eating.

Again, notice the feeling of the food in your mouth, on your teeth, on your tongue, on your lips.

Chew until the food is completely ready to be swallowed.

Swallow. Pay attention to how the food feels as it leaves your mouth and slides down your throat. Notice how far down it goes before you can't feel it anymore. Notice if there is any food still in your mouth or if it's empty now.

Tune in to how your stomach feels. Notice how it feels different after you have eaten a little food and then after you have eaten a lot of food.

Repeat this process until your food is gone or until you feel full.

Visit http://www.newharbinger.com/36255 to download an audio version of this mindful eating process.

making healthy choices 33
about drugs and alcohol

for you to know

Many teens experiment with drugs and alcohol. Having ADHD increases the risk of substance abuse. You can make healthy choices about using drugs or alcohol by understanding your reasons for using and the consequences of using on your body and on your life. You can use a mindfulness skill to help you calm yourself and focus without the use of substances.

Brandon hung around with some friends who were encouraging him to try alcohol. He knew it probably wasn't a good thing for him to be doing, but he wasn't exactly sure why. He struggled to figure out how to handle their pressure to use. His therapist helped him explore his feelings about using and learn more about the effects of drugs and alcohol on his brain and body. He knew he needed to make good choices, and he was surprised to learn that having ADHD increased his risk of abusing substances. Once he realized how using alcohol with his friends might impact his life, he made a decision to remain drug- and alcohol-free and simply told his friends, "No thanks." He noticed over time that he tended to hang out more often with friends who were not drinking alcohol.

Eric had been using marijuana for a while now. He felt that it calmed him, decreased his ADHD symptoms, and made him feel more normal. He had started out using just once in a while but noticed that he was using more and more often lately. He sometimes worried about what his marijuana use was doing to his brain. He noticed that his motivation to do things had all but disappeared since he started using. And he was having more and more trouble remembering things. He also worried that his parents would find out. And he knew his soccer coach would throw him off the team if he knew he was getting high.

His therapist encouraged him to explore what he liked and disliked about using marijuana. He helped him make a list of the pros and cons of using. Eric thought he could just cut down on how often he used but discovered that didn't work for him. He wanted the benefit of using but decided he would rather find ways to calm and center himself other than using marijuana.

His therapist taught him a mindfulness skill he could use to decrease his urge to use, to calm himself, and to help him focus without the use of drugs or alcohol. After Eric started practicing this skill whenever he felt the urge to use marijuana, he found that he was able to tune in and calm himself without using. And he noticed that his urge to use was gradually decreasing until eventually he wasn't using at all. A few weeks after his last use, he noticed that a kind of mental fog had cleared from his brain, a fog that he hadn't even noticed while he was using.

for you to do

In order to make healthy choices about drug and alcohol use, it helps to be mindful of why you might use, the effects of the substance on your body, and the potentially negative consequences of using on your life. If you drink or use drugs or have ever been tempted to do so, answer the following questions to help yourself think about how using might impact your life. If you are uncomfortable writing your answers, simply answer the questions in your head or talk about them with a trusted family member, friend, or therapist.

Are you ever tempted to drink or use drugs, and if so, what?

_____

_____

_____

If you drink alcohol or use drugs, list what you use, as well as how often and how much.

_____

_____

_____

_____

_____

Search online for the effects of the substance you use (or are tempted to use) on your body and brain and describe them here.

_____

_____

_____

_____

_____

If your friends use drugs or alcohol, describe what they use, how much, and how often.

_____

_____

_____

_____

_____

How do you feel when your friends use?

_____

_____

_____

What positive or negative effects do you see that substance use has on your friends' lives?

_____

_____

_____

_____

_____

Do you feel peer pressure to use? If so, how do you deal with it?

_____

_____

_____

What do you like about using?

_____

_____

_____

_____

_____

What don't you like about using?

_____

_____

_____

_____

_____

How does using affect your ADHD symptoms?

_____

_____

_____

_____

How do you think using is helpful to you?

_____

_____

_____

_____

_____

How do you think using is unhelpful to you?

_____

_____

_____

_____

_____

What are the possible negative consequences of using and how would you deal with them?

_____

_____

_____

_____

If you experience cravings, what triggers them? How do you handle them?

_____

_____

_____

_____

What are your personal risk factors for substance abuse (for example, ADHD, a family member with addiction)?

_____

_____

_____

_____

_____

Do you ever worry that you have a substance-abuse problem? If so, what triggers your worry?

_____

_____

_____

_____

_____

Have you ever tried unsuccessfully to stop using? If so, describe what happened.

_____

_____

_____

_____

_____

Do you use alone?

_____

_____

_____

Who do you use with?

_____

_____

_____

Describe how you decide whether or not to drink or use drugs.

_____

_____

_____

What changes do you need to make in your choices to use drugs or alcohol?

_____

_____

_____

_____

... and more to do

Whenever you are tempted to use drugs or alcohol, you can use this process to calm and center yourself until the temptation or craving goes away.

Quiet your mind and body and go within.

Take a slow deep breath in through your nose to the count of four, and exhale through your mouth to the count of eight.

Do it again. Breathe in to the count of four and breathe out to the count of eight.

Think about your intentions for success in your life.

Spend a moment thinking about how using drugs or alcohol might get in the way of your success. Be specific.

Think about the effects of the substance on your body and on your brain.

Consider the risk of addiction and loss of control. How does using impact your ability to make good decisions? How might using damage your relationships? How does being high or drunk interfere with work or school? Could using get you in trouble with the law?

Tune in to your body.

Now notice everything there is to notice about how your body feels.

What does a craving feel like to you in your body?

How does your mind feel?

Imagine that the craving is like a wave that comes to shore. Just observe the feeling of the craving wave.

Notice how it comes to shore and then recedes back out to sea.

Feel the rhythm of the ebb and flow of the waves.

Imagine that you are surfing the urge to use.

Remind yourself that your urge will lessen and then come again, lessen and come again, much like the waves come to shore and then go back out.

Just let the craving come and go. There is no need to act on it.

Trust that your craving will gradually lessen until it goes away.

Visit http://www.newharbinger.com/36255 to download an audio version of this process that you can use to handle cravings and lessen your desire to use drugs or alcohol.

for you to know

As a group, teen drivers have a high accident rate. For teens with ADHD, symptoms such as distractibility and impulsivity can make this even worse. You can use mindfulness exercises to help you focus on driving, filter out distractions, and pay attention to what is most important while driving.

Caleb loved to drive, but he was embarrassed by the fact that he had already had two significant accidents that were his fault. Thankfully no one had been hurt. He knew he got distracted sometimes while he was driving, but he wasn't sure what to do about it.

Caleb's ADHD coach explored the details of Caleb's accidents with him and discovered that both times Caleb had been distracted—once by reading a text on his cell phone and once by a friend who was riding with him. His coach helped Caleb explore how to reduce possible distractions and taught him a process for keeping his mind focused on driving.

for you to do

Answer the following questions to help you be mindful of what you need to pay attention to while driving and to help you decrease distractions. Then review your answers in your head before driving to remind yourself to drive mindfully.

What is the most important thing to pay attention to when you are driving?

_____

_____

What do you think about while you are driving?

_____

_____

What should you be focused on while you are driving?

_____

_____

How can you remind yourself to pay attention to driving and nothing else while driving?

_____

_____

Where should you be looking while driving?

_____

_____

What distracts you while driving?

_____

_____

How can you deal with your cell phone so it does not distract you while driving? (Examples: place in driving mode, turn off the volume, pull over safely before looking at texts or answering phone)

_____

_____

How can you select music safely?

_____

_____

When you drive with friends in the car, what can you do to help make sure they do not distract you?

_____

_____

... and more to do

Practice the following "How to Drive Mindfully" process, first in your imagination and then while you are driving. This will help you stay focused on what's most important while driving.

When you first get into the car, notice how it feels to sit in the driver's seat. Notice how the seat feels against your back and bottom. Is it soft, firm, or cushiony? Do you need to move it to comfortably reach the gas pedal, or is it just right?

Before you start the car, adjust your cell phone so it will not make any sound that distracts you while driving. Set your intention to pay attention to driving and only driving and to ignore the phone until you arrive at your destination or to pull over safely before you pay attention to it.

Pay attention to the feel of the steering wheel as you grasp it with your hands and fingers. Is it warm, cold, hard, soft, smooth, slippery, or sticky?

Put the key in the ignition and start the car. How does the car sound? Is it running smoothly or misfiring?

Notice the gas gauge. Make sure you have enough gas, and if not, plan to fill up promptly.

As you prepare to pull out of the parking space, check for other cars all the way around you, and wait for a clear space.

As you pull out onto the road, look out the front window and notice what you see. Do you see other cars? Is there a lot of traffic? What type of road are you driving on?

Pay attention to the other cars as they come into your view, as they go by in the other direction, and as they travel beside you on a four-lane road.

Check the rearview and side mirrors quickly, and keep your eyes on the road. Notice the cars, pedestrians, bicycles, or anything else that is sharing the road or might be pulling onto the road.

Be alert for anything that requires you to change speed or direction.

As soon as you realize that you are not thinking about driving, just acknowledge the fact and return your attention to driving. You might repeat the words "I'm driving, I'm driving" to help you stay focused.

Notice the traffic signs, the traffic lights, and the markings on the road. Notice the cars that are near you.

Keep your eyes and your attention on the road.

If your mind wanders, bring your awareness briefly back to the feel of the steering wheel. Notice how it feels now that you have been holding on to it for a while. Use the feel of the steering wheel to anchor your attention on the task of driving.

Repeat, "I'm driving, I'm driving."

Continually check the mirrors, and keep your eyes on the road and your awareness on the task of driving until you arrive at your destination.

Reflect on the experience of being mindful while driving. How far did you get before you realized you weren't thinking about driving? What worked best to get your attention back on driving and to keep it there?

Visit http://www.newharbinger.com/36255 to download an audio version of this process that you can use to practice the process of driving mindfully. Listen several times until you can remember and do the process while you are driving. Do not listen while driving.

Section 5

Creating Success

Some teens are busy preparing for college, others for employment. This section helps you explore what you want to accomplish and set a positive intention for success. It guides you through the process of finding and succeeding at a job, mentally rehearsing your desired success, and planning your future.

35 setting your intention to succeed

for you to know

Some teens with ADHD become discouraged and disheartened because they try so hard to succeed, only to have their ADHD symptoms get in their way of achieving success. Setting your intention is an essential first step in creating success in any area of your life.

Loren wished she could do a better job in school and at her part-time job. She frequently felt discouraged because she tried so hard but often got distracted, forgot to do things, and was behind in her schoolwork. At her job at a local ice cream shop, customers complained when she talked to her friends too long at the counter or forgot what they ordered. She knew she needed to change something, but she wasn't sure what.

Her ADHD coach asked Loren to list the things she wanted to be successful at doing. Next he asked her to write down what got in her way of success. Then he taught her a mindfulness process she could use to set her intention to succeed. Once she wrote down the things she wanted to succeed at, she remembered to set her intention whenever she was doing something on the list. She discovered that she stayed on task, was less distracted, and created more success in her life when she used the mindfulness process to set her intention to succeed with schoolwork, at her job, and at anything else she wanted to do well.

for you to do

List from five to ten things you want to succeed at. Be specific. Include everyday tasks, like getting your homework done on time, as well as long-term goals, such as getting into a good college.

_____

_____

_____

_____

_____

_____

_____

For the three most important items on your list, answer these three questions:

My intention: _____

Why do I want to do this?

_____

_____

_____

What will I accomplish if I do this?

_____

_____

_____

activity 35 ✳ setting your intention to succeed

What is the purpose of this intention?

_____

_____

_____

My intention: _____

Why do I want to do this?

_____

_____

_____

What will I accomplish if I do this?

_____

_____

_____

What is the purpose of this intention?

_____

_____

_____

My intention: _____

Why do I want to do this?

_____

_____

_____

What will I accomplish if I do this?

_____

_____

_____

What is the purpose of this intention?

_____

_____

_____

Describe how your ADHD symptoms impact your success with the things on your list. Be specific. (Examples: My impulsivity led me to choose to hang out with friends at the last minute instead of doing my homework last night; I got distracted by my favorite online game when I was supposed to be doing my homework; I was not organized and missed a deadline for getting my college applications submitted; I got my report done on time because I was able to hyperfocus.)

_____

_____

_____

_____

_____

_____

_____

_____

... and more to do

Practice the following mindfulness of intention for success process to increase your success rate. Go over the process in your imagination every day, and use it whenever you are doing something you want to succeed at doing.

Take a slow deep breath and exhale slowly.

Bring to mind something you want to be more successful at doing.

Set your intention to do it successfully.

How will you know you have succeeded?

Picture yourself doing the task or activity you have chosen.

What do you need to do to be successful?

In your mind's eye, see yourself doing the task or activity very successfully.

Feel what it feels like when you are successful.

Notice distractions that might get in your way of success.

Dismiss the distractions, and remind yourself of your intention to succeed.

Visualize yourself staying on task.

Pay attention to what you need to do to succeed.

Stay focused.

Every few minutes, notice what you are doing and ask yourself if it is helping or hindering your success.

Bring your attention back to what you need to be doing to succeed.

Do this over and over until you succeed.

You will find an audio recording of this meditation online at http://www.newharbinger .com/36255.

mentally rehearsing for success 36

for you to know

Teens are involved in many activities where they desire to be successful. Those with ADHD often encounter extra challenges, as their poor concentration, distractibility, and impulsiveness may interfere with their success. You can mentally rehearse your activities to help you create your desired outcome. Athletes, performers, executives, writers, and others at the top of their field use this technique to create what they want to achieve.

Justin loved playing sports. Now that he was a sophomore in high school, he had narrowed down his interest to baseball. He thought he might even like to play professionally someday. But his performance was inconsistent. Some days he was the star of the team. Other days he felt embarrassed and disgusted with himself when he missed hitting perfect pitches or didn't throw the ball to the right place in time.

His therapist asked Justin if there were any other areas of his life where his performance was inconsistent. He realized that it happened with his schoolwork and even with his friendships. Together they explored how his ADHD might be impacting his consistency. His therapist shared a process that Justin could use to prepare and mentally rehearse success. He explained that mental rehearsal is a process people can use when they want to practice doing something ahead of time to visualize and create success.

He explained that our brains really don't know the difference between actually doing a specific activity and imagining doing the activity and that by mentally rehearsing we can teach our brains to be more efficient, which will increase our success.

When Justin practiced the process before a game, he noticed that his play became more consistently solid. He also discovered that he got better grades and got along better with people when he used the process to mentally rehearse success at school and with relationships.

for you to do

The first step in creating success for yourself is to identify what you want to be successful at.

List from five to ten things you would like to be more successful at doing. Be specific.

_____   _____

_____   _____

_____   _____

_____   _____

_____   _____

Explain how your life would be different if you were successful at each of these things.

_____

_____

_____

_____

_____

_____

_____

_____

To help you succeed at each of these things, what would you be doing differently than you do now? (Example: To succeed at getting a better grade in math, I would be doing all my homework and turning it in on time, studying for every test, and asking for help with things I don't understand.)

_____

_____

_____

_____

_____

_____

_____

... and more to do

You can use the following mental rehearsal process to succeed in anything you choose, such as school, preparing for an exam, getting into college, having great relationships, or doing your best in sports, music, dance, or at work. For maximum benefit, use this process twice each day, including during the five minutes right before you go to sleep. When you use it before sleep, you infuse your subconscious with the powerful success messages, which may increase the effectiveness of the process. After you use this process, start looking for evidence that success is starting to show up for you.

What do you want to achieve right now? Choose it and start to picture it in your mind.

Close your eyes and take a slow deep breath in through your nose and exhale slowly through your mouth, like you are blowing a huge bubble.

Do it again. Inhale slowly and deeply and then blow out slowly and gently.

Again, picture in your mind what it is that you want to succeed at.

Imagine that you are doing it now.

Pretend you are doing everything that is involved in it.

Notice what you are doing that helps you perform at your absolute peak.

You are doing it so well.

Feel what it feels like to be doing it effortlessly and successfully. How does it feel?

Notice how it feels in your mind.

Notice what it feels like in your body. Where do you feel it?

If any doubt arises about your ability, just acknowledge the doubt, and tell yourself, *There is no need for doubt right now. I'm performing at my absolute peak. I am succeeding.*

If you get distracted, that's okay; just bring your attention back to imagining everything there is to imagine about doing what you want to do, and about doing it expertly.

Picture each step of the process in every detail. Imagine the surroundings, the sounds, the smells, the people involved.

See it and experience it as if you are there doing it right now. Feel what it feels like to be successful.

Your brain doesn't know the difference between imagining you are doing it and actually doing it.

Everything is flowing effortlessly. Your mind is sharp and quick. You know everything you need to know. All your hard work, study, and practice are paying off for you.

Your body is in perfect condition, responding exactly as you need it to. It knows what to do and how to do it without conscious thought.

Your mind is programmed exactly as it needs to be from your practice, your visualization, and your conditioning.

You are doing this.

Use the power of your imagination to picture and create success.

Imagine it, feel it, create it.

Look for evidence that success is showing up in your daily life.

And so it is.

Visit http://www.newharbinger.com/36255 to download an audio version of this process that you can use to mentally rehearse anything you want to be successful at.

37 finding a part-time job

for you to know

Teens typically become interested in working when they become old enough to work. Teens with ADHD need to be mindful of choosing a job where their ADHD symptoms boost their performance rather than hindering it. Being mindful of what skills and interests you can offer a potential employer will assist you in gaining employment where you can enjoy the work and be successful.

Emma wanted to find a part-time job. She had just turned sixteen, and many of her friends had already started working. She thought she would enjoy having some spending money and liked the idea of saving for her college expenses. The only thing was, she had no idea what kind of work she wanted to do, and she worried that she wasn't qualified to do anything since she had never worked. She also worried about how her ADHD might impact her work performance and wanted to find a job where her challenges with being easily distracted, having trouble keeping track of time, and being quite disorganized wouldn't interfere with her ability to succeed at work.

Emma's ADHD coach helped her explore her interests and skills that might be applied to various work situations. She wrote down what she thought she would be doing in an ideal job that was designed just for her. Then she made a list of things she liked to do and another list of things she felt she was good at. She thought about work where her ADHD symptoms might be helpful to her and realized that her ADHD might make some jobs more difficult for her. Her high energy and love of people steered her away from a sedentary desk job, where she wouldn't talk with others every day, and toward jobs that were fast paced and required lots of interaction.

Emma used several online job-search websites and printed out local jobs that looked like they involved frequent interaction with people and where she could be helpful and physically active. She eventually chose to apply for more than ten different jobs that had these attributes, such as wait staff at the local pizza parlor, aide at an after-school child care program, cashier at a grocery store, and working at the front desk at the local YMCA.

for you to do

Describe exactly what you would be doing in your ideal job. Be specific. Include your responsibilities, tasks, hours, location, setting, and coworkers. Think of jobs you know about in fields such as retail, food service, education, camps, computers, automotive, or science, as well as any that you have a particular interest in learning more about. To help you with this, ask friends and family what they do at their jobs.

_____

_____

_____

_____

_____

_____

_____

Make a list of your interests, including things you would like to learn more about.

_____

_____

_____

_____

_____

_____

_____

Make a list of your skills or things you are good at. If you can't think of any, ask for help from your parents or teachers.

_____

_____

_____

_____

_____

_____

_____

Make a list of skills you've used as a volunteer or with your family.

_____

_____

_____

_____

_____

_____

_____

Go online and learn about the tasks involved in doing ten different jobs that look interesting to you. Write down what the jobs are and list three skills needed for each one.

_____

_____

_____

_____

_____

_____

_____

_____

_____

_____

_____

_____

_____

_____

_____

_____

_____

_____

_____

_____

_____

... and more to do

Being mindful of how your ADHD symptoms impact your work performance can help you choose a job that is a good fit for you. Following a process to organize your job search will improve your chances of finding a suitable job and getting hired.

Describe types of jobs where your ADHD symptoms might help you succeed.

_____

_____

_____

_____

_____

Describe types of jobs where your ADHD symptoms might hinder your success.

_____

_____

_____

_____

_____

Do an online search for part-time jobs in your geographic area that might be a good fit for you. Think about your skills, your interests, and how your ADHD might impact your job performance in each situation. Notice the experience required and the working hours required.

Ask family, teachers, and friends if they know of any job openings that match what you are looking for. Notice "Help Wanted" signs wherever you go, and ask for an application.

Using the chart below (which you can download at http://www.newharbinger.com/36255), list ten jobs that look like they meet your criteria. Submit applications for these ten jobs either online or in person. Write down the date you submitted the application, as well as the contact information you will need to follow up on your application.

One week after you submit each application, follow up with the potential employer to make sure they received your application and to check the status of it.

Job	Date of application	Contact information	Date of follow up	Status

Repeat the follow-up process until you get an interview and find a job. Be sure to send a thank-you note after each interview.

If necessary, search for more jobs to add to your list, and follow the application and follow-up process until you find a job that works for you.

38 role-playing the interview

for you to know

A job interview can be anxiety provoking. Preparing yourself to answer commonly asked questions as well as role-playing a job interview can help you do your best during the actual interview.

Logan wanted to get a part-time job. After applying for more than ten jobs and following up with phone calls, he was invited to come in for an interview with one of the potential employers, the manager at a pizza parlor. Logan had never interviewed for a job before, and he felt really anxious about it.

Logan's therapist helped him explore why he felt so anxious about the interview. After he asked Logan some questions often asked in a first interview, his therapist pretended to be the interviewer so he and Logan could role-play what the interview might be like. Logan struggled to answer some of the questions at first, but after giving them some thought he came up with honest, positive responses that showed the interviewer how he could be an asset to the employer. He felt prepared and confident during his interview.

for you to do

Based on a job you have identified as one you would like to get, write down the answers to the following questions that are often asked during a job interview so you will be prepared to answer them during an actual interview.

How did you hear about this job?

_____

_____

_____

Why do you want to work here?

_____

_____

_____

What do you know about this company or business?

_____

_____

_____

Have you ever worked before?

_____

_____

_____

Tell me about yourself.

_____

_____

_____

activity 38 ✳ role-playing the interview

What skills do you have?

_____

_____

_____

Why should I hire you?

_____

_____

_____

How do people describe you?

_____

_____

_____

Where do you see yourself in five years?

_____

_____

_____

What is your greatest strength?

_____

_____

_____

What is your greatest weakness?

_____

_____

_____

Describe a time you made a mistake, and explain what you did to correct it.

_____

_____

_____

How well do you interact with people?

_____

_____

_____

Describe a conflict you had and how you resolved it.

_____

_____

_____

What hours can you work?

_____

_____

_____

What do you want to know about this job?

_____

_____

_____

What do you want to know about the person who would be your boss?

_____

_____

_____

... and more to do

After you answer the sample interview questions above, ask someone (perhaps a friend, parent, teacher, or therapist) to be the interviewer as you role-play a job interview. Share the questions listed above so the person can ask you to answer them. Pick one of the jobs you applied for, and answer the questions as if you were being interviewed for that job. Make this fun, but be sure to be mindful of what skills the job needs and how you are a good fit for the job.

for you to know

In order to be successful at work, you need to be mindful of the tasks and responsibilities required by the position and the employer. Taking time to be clear on your work schedule and exactly what is expected of you will help you stay organized and on task.

Ryan was thrilled when he was hired to work as a janitor at a local gym. The pay was good, and he could work after school and still have time to do his homework. He even got free gym time! But by the end of the first week he felt stressed out, and he knew his boss was unhappy with him. He had totally missed a shift assigned to him. And he had forgotten to empty the garbage can in the lobby twice.

Ryan's ADHD job coach suggested that he use the calendar app on his phone to enter in his work schedule each week as soon as it was posted. Ryan set up an alarm to remind him ahead of time when he needed to be at work so he could get there in time. Then the coach encouraged Ryan to talk to his boss to make sure he knew exactly what he was supposed to do each day.

Ryan made a list of his job tasks and responsibilities and entered it into the reminder app on his phone so he would have a checklist he could refer to every day. When his boss added some new responsibilities, Ryan added them to his checklist. Each evening he checked his calendar to see when he needed to be at work the next day. When he arrived at work, he looked over his task list and checked off each item as he completed it.

After Ryan had worked for a month, his boss told him he was very pleased with how well he got everything done and the fact that he arrived a few minutes early for his work shift every day. Ryan felt good about his job and how well he was doing.

for you to do

Create a system for yourself to keep track of your work schedule, job tasks, and responsibilities.

Work schedule: Check it as soon as it's available and enter it into your calendar app. Write it down here for the first two weeks.

_____

_____

_____

_____

_____

_____

Job tasks: Ask your boss for a list of tasks you are expected to do. (Examples: answer the phone, take phone orders, give orders to the kitchen, wait on customers, use the cash register to take customer payment) Make sure you have a clear understanding of what tasks you are supposed to do and how and when to do them. List them here:

_____

_____

_____

_____

_____

_____

_____

_____

Your responsibilities: What are you responsible for in this job? Perhaps you are responsible for making sure the dining room is clean at the end of the night shift. This might include the tasks of checking to see that the tables have been wiped down and reset, the floor vacuumed, and the trash emptied.

_____

_____

_____

_____

_____

_____

_____

_____

_____

... and more to do

Before you fall asleep each night, use the following process to prepare yourself for the next day's work.

Close your eyes and go within.

Take a deep breath in through your nose to the count of four and exhale through your mouth to the count of eight.

Take a moment to review in your mind's eye all the good things that happened during the day.

Make a mental list of things that happened today that you are grateful for.

Now bring your attention to tomorrow.

What time do you need to be up in the morning?

What is on your schedule for the day?

Picture yourself doing all the activities and tasks scheduled for the day.

Notice what time you need to be at work.

See yourself arriving everywhere you need to be a few minutes early.

What does it feel like to be early?

Imagine that you are at work.

Review your job responsibilities in your mind.

Think about what you will do at work tomorrow.

Imagine yourself doing everything you need to do at work.

Think about what you need to pay attention to, and imagine you are paying attention to that.

Notice what you feel like when you stay focused on the most important thing.

Be mindful of what distracts you from doing your job.

Notice when you are distracted, and bring your attention back to the task you need to be focused on.

Is there anything you have forgotten about that you need to do?

Is there anything you need help with or that you don't understand about your work?

If so, imagine that you are asking for help and getting what you need.

Picture yourself using your calendar and reminder apps to keep yourself organized and to get things done on time.

Notice how it feels to do your job successfully and on time.

Now that you have mentally prepared yourself for work, relax and go to sleep knowing you have programmed your brain for a successful day at work.

You will find an audio recording of this online at http://www.newharbinger.com/36255.

40 planning for your future

for you to know

Teens often feel stressed when they think about what they want to do after high school. You may worry about choosing a career that fits your strengths, your needs, and your style. You may wonder how to take your ADHD into account when planning your future. Being mindful of your dreams, passions, interests, and skills will help you create a satisfying and successful future.

Alex felt stressed out and anxious whenever he thought about what he wanted to do after high school. He thought he should go to college, but he struggled academically and really hated school, and he worried that college would just be more of the same for him. He wondered if there were other options.

Vanessa couldn't wait to graduate and go to college, but she was overwhelmed with the process of figuring out what she wanted to study and to do for a career. She worried that she would make a poor choice and would waste her time. She sometimes wondered what kind of career she was suited for since her ADHD symptoms often got in her way.

Alex and Vanessa's therapist suggested that they talk with their guidance counselors to help them identify their strengths, weaknesses, and interests through testing. Then he asked them to write down what they were interested in doing and what they might be truly passionate about. He suggested that Alex and Vanessa do some research into careers that used their unique set of strengths and skills and that might be a good fit for them. He also recommended that they search online for lists of careers that were a good fit for those with ADHD to maximize their success. Then he taught them a mindfulness visualization technique they could use to picture and create their future.

for you to do

Ask your school guidance counselor if you have taken any tests that measure your strengths, weaknesses, and interests that might help in choosing a career, or where you might take one if you haven't done so.

If available, review the test results and write down ten things that come out on top.

1. _____
2. _____
3. _____
4. _____
5. _____

6. _____
7. _____
8. _____
9. _____
10. _____

Ask your parents and teachers what they think your strengths and skills are. Write down ten of these here.

1. _____
2. _____
3. _____
4. _____
5. _____

6. _____
7. _____
8. _____
9. _____
10. _____

activity 40 * planning for your future

List ten things you love to do.

1. _____   6. _____

2. _____   7. _____

3. _____   8. _____

4. _____   9. _____

5. _____   10. _____

List ten of your best skills.

1. _____   6. _____

2. _____   7. _____

3. _____   8. _____

4. _____   9. _____

5. _____   10. _____

List ten of your favorite interests.

1. _____   6. _____

2. _____   7. _____

3. _____   8. _____

4. _____   9. _____

5. _____   10. _____

Describe something you are passionate about.

_____
_____
_____
_____
_____

What have you always dreamed of doing?

_____
_____
_____
_____
_____

As a child, what did you tell yourself you wanted to be when you grew up?

_____
_____
_____
_____

Research the types of careers or professions that involve your skills and interests. Write down ten that match.

1. _____   6. _____

2. _____   7. _____

3. _____   8. _____

4. _____   9. _____

5. _____   10. _____

activity 40 ✳ planning for your future

Research careers and professions that are a good fit for someone with ADHD. Write down ten that interest you.

1. _____   6. _____

2. _____   7. _____

3. _____   8. _____

4. _____   9. _____

5. _____   10. _____

Find out and describe the training or preparation that is needed for the ten careers you listed.

1. _____   6. _____

2. _____   7. _____

3. _____   8. _____

4. _____   9. _____

5. _____   10. _____

... and more to do

Use the following process to imagine and create the future you desire.

Close your eyes. Take a deep breath in, and relax your mind as you exhale.

Inhale again, and as you exhale relax your body.

Be still and go within.

Now imagine a future time when you are an adult.

You have graduated from high school and completed preparation for your career, no matter how long it took.

Picture everything possible about what your life is like.

Where do you live?

What does your home look like?

Who lives with you?

Where do you work?

What do you like most about your work?

How satisfied are you with your work?

What skills do you use at work?

Are you passionate about your work?

How do you feel about your work?

How does ADHD help you succeed at work?

How does ADHD interfere with your work?

How did you train or prepare for your work?

What is the most important thing in your life?

How much money do you earn?

Are you married or single?

Are you a parent?

If you could go back and change something about your life, what, if anything, would you change?

Slowly return your attention to the present moment.

Use this process periodically to tune in to what you really want to do with your life and work.

Visit http://www.newharbinger.com/36255 to download an audio version of this process.

An Ending Note to Teens

I'm delighted that you have worked through so many of the activities. You now know many new mindfulness skills that you can use to be successful for the rest of your life. I recommend that you post a list of the activities that helped you the most where you can see it every day to remind you to keep practicing the skills. As with any new skill, the more you practice, the better you will get and the more benefit you will notice.

Best wishes on your mindful journey through your amazing life!

Acknowledgments

This book is a culmination of thirty years of practicing mindfulness, raising a daughter with ADHD, and helping thousands of clients thrive and succeed with ADHD. My journey into the universe of ADHD began when my daughter, Jen, was diagnosed. I thank her from the depths of my heart for teaching me that although ADHD can make some things more challenging, it can also offer tremendous gifts of creativity, energy, love, and joy.

My deepest thanks to Wendy Millstine from New Harbinger Publications, who invited me to write this workbook and who has guided, supported, and encouraged me along the way. Many thanks to all those at New Harbinger who have read and reread, edited, and helped me create and shape this workbook.

Thank you to all my clients with ADHD for sharing their journeys with me and for teaching me not only about their challenges but also how to embrace and thrive with ADHD.

And thanks to my amazing husband, Al, with whom I share a new life full of love, play, connection, and mindful happiness. Life is good!

References

American Psychiatric Association, 2013. *Diagnostic and Statistical Manual of Mental Disorders, 5th Edition: DSM-5*. Washington, DC: Author.

Benson, H. 2000. *The Relaxation Response*. (Updated). New York: William Morrow Paperbacks.

Biegel, G, K. Brown, S. Shapiro, and C. Schubert. 2009. "Mindfulness-Based Stress Reduction for the Treatment of Adolescent Psychiatric Outpatients: A Randomized Clinical Trial." *Journal of Consulting and Clinical Psychology* 77: 855–866.

Blackman, G., R. Ostrander, and K. Herman. 2005. "Children with ADHD and Depression: A Multisource, Multimethod Assessment of Clinical, Social, and Academic Functioning." *Journal of Attention Disorders* 8: 195–207.

Burdick, D. 2014. *Mindfulness Skills for Kids and Teens: A Workbook for Clinicians and Clients with 154 Tools, Techniques, Activities and Worksheets*. Eau Claire, WI: PESI Publishing and Media.

——. 2015. *ADHD: Non-Medication Treatments and Skills for Children and Teens. A Workbook for Clinicians and Parents with 162 Tools, Techniques, Activities and Handouts*. Eau Claire, WI: PESI Publishing and Media.

Burke, C. 2009. "Mindfulness-Based Approaches with Children and Adolescents: A Preliminary Review of Current Research in an Emergent Field." *Journal of Child and Family Studies*. Online DOI 10.1007/s10826–009–9282-x.

Cooper-Kahn, J., and L. Dietzel. 2008. *Late, Lost, and Unprepared*. Bethesda, MD: Woodbine House.

Cortese, S., E. Konofal, N. Yateman, M. Mouren, and M. Lecendreux. 2006. "Sleep and Alertness in Children with Attention-Deficit/Hyperactivity Disorder: A Systematic Review of the Literature." *Sleep: Journal of Sleep and Sleep Disorders* 29: 504–511.

Dalai Lama. 2001. *An Open Heart: Practicing Compassion in Everyday Life*. New York: Little, Brown and Company.

De Boo, G. M., and P. J. Prins. 2007. "Social Incompetence in Children with ADHD: Possible Moderators and Mediators in Social-Skills Training." *Clinical Psychology Review* 27: 78–97.

Earley, J., and B. Weiss. 2010. *Self-Therapy for Your Inner Critic: Transforming Self-Criticism into Self-Confidence*. Larkspur, CA: Pattern System Books.

Efron, L., and P. Pearl. 2001. "Sleep Disorders in Children with ADHD." *ADVANCE for Respiratory Care Practitioners, 14,* Retrieved Jan 15, 2003, from: http://respiratory-care-sleep-medicine.advanceweb.com/Article/Sleep-Disorders-in-Children-with-ADHD.aspx.

Ewing, J. 1984. "Detecting Alcoholism: The CAGE Questionnaire." *Journal of the American Medical Association* 252: 1905–7.

Farb, N. A. S., Z. V. Segal, H. Mayberg, J. Bean, D. McKeon, Z. Fatima, and A. K. Anderson. 2007. "Attending to the Present: Mindfulness Meditation Reveals Distinct Neural Modes of Self-Reference." *Social Cognitive and Affective Neuroscience* 2: 313–322.

Flook, L., S. L. Smalley, M. J. Kitil, B. M. Galla, S. Kaiser-Greenland, J. Locke, E. Ishijima, and C. Kasari. 2010. "Effects of Mindful Awareness Practices on Executive Functions in Elementary School Children." *Journal of Applied School Psychology* 26: 70–95.

Hallowell, E., and J. Ratey. 2005. *Delivered from Distraction.* New York: Ballantine Books.

Hawn Foundation. 2011. *The MindUP Curriculum, Grades Pre-K–2.* New York: Scholastic Inc.

Hölzel, B. K., U. Ott, T. Gard, H. Hempel, M. Weygandt, K. Morgen, and D. Vaitl. 2007. "Investigation of Mindfulness Meditation Practitioners with Voxel-Based Morphometry." *Social Cognitive and Affective Neuroscience* 3: 55–61.

Honos-Webb, L. 2010. *The Gift of ADHD: How to Transform Your Child's Problems into Strengths.* Oakland, CA: New Harbinger Publications, Inc.

——. 2010. *The ADHD Workbook For Teens.* Oakland, CA: New Harbinger Publications, Inc.

Hooker, K., and I. Fodor. 2008. "Teaching Mindfulness to Children." *Gestalt Review* 12: 75–91.

Hutcherson, C. A., E. M. Seppala, and J. J. Gross. "I Don't Know You But I Like You: Loving Kindness Meditation Increases Positivity Toward Others." Paper presented at the Sixth Annual Conference Integrating Mindfulness-Based Interventions into Medicine, Worcester, MA: *Health Care and Society;* 2008.

Jha, A. P. 2005. "Garrison Institute Report: Contemplation and Education: Scientific Research Issues Relevant to School-Based Contemplative Programs: A Supplement." New York: Garrison Institute.

Kabat-Zinn, J. 2003. "Mindfulness-Based Interventions in Context: Past, Present, and Future." *Clinical Psychology: Science and Practice* 10: 144–156.

Kaiser-Greenland, S. 2010. *The Mindful Child.* New York: Free Press.

Linden, W. 1973. "Practicing of Meditation by School Children and Their Levels of Field Dependence-Independence, Test Anxiety, and Reading Achievement." *Journal of Consulting and Clinical Psychology* 41: 139–143.

Mazzone, L, V. Postorino, L. Reale, M. Guarnera, V. Mannino, M. Armando, L. Fatta, L. DePeppo, and S. Vicarii. "Self-Esteem Evaluation in Children and Adolescents Suffering from ADHD." *Clinical Practice and Epidemiology in Mental Health* 9: 96–102. doi:10.2174/1745017901309010096 .

Napoli, M., P. R. Krech, and L. Holley. 2005. "Mindfulness Training for Elementary School Students: The Attention Academy." *Journal of Applied School Psychology* 21: 99–125.

National Association of School Psychologists. 2002. "Social Skills: Promoting Positive Behavior, Academic Success, and School Safety." Retrieved Feb. 6, 2015 from: http://www.naspcenter.org/factsheets/socialskills_fs.html

Nhat Hanh, Thich. 2008. *Mindful Movements.* Berkeley, CA: Parallax Press.

——. 2011. *Planting Seeds: Practicing Mindfulness with Children.* Berkeley, CA: Parallax Press.

Omizo, M. M., and W. B. Michael. 1982. "Biofeedback-Induced Relaxation Training and Impulsivity, Attention to Task, and Locus of Control Among Hyperactive Boys." *Journal of Learning Disabilities* 15: 414–416.

Ott, M. J. 2002. "Mindfulness Meditation in Pediatric Clinical Practice." *Pediatric Nursing* 28: 487–491.

Preston, S. DTLA-4: *Detroit Test of Learning Aptitude.* Fourth Edition. Available at: http://www.slosson.com/onlinecatalogstore_i1003126.html?catId=51515

Rivera, E., and M. M. Omizo. 1980. "The Effects of Relaxation and Biofeedback on Attention to Task and Impulsivity Among Male Hyperactive Children." *The Exceptional Child* 27: 41–51.

Saltzman, A. (2011). "Mindfulness: A Guide for Teachers." Retrieved Nov. 6, 2016 from http://www.contemplativemind.org/Mindfulness-A_Teachers_Guide.pdf

Schonert-Reichl, K., and M. Lawlor. 2010. "The Effects of a Mindfulness-Based Education Program on Pre- and Early Adolescents' Well-Being and Social and Emotional Competence." *Mindfulness* 1: 137–151.

Semple, R. J., J. Lee, and L. F. Miller. 2006. "Mindfulness-Based Cognitive Therapy for Children." In *Mindfulness-Based Treatment Approaches: Clinician's Guide to Evidence Base and Applications,* edited by R. A. Baer. Oxford, UK: Elsevier.

Semple, R. J., E. Reid, and L. Miller. 2005. "Treating Anxiety with Mindfulness: An Open Trial of Mindfulness Training for Anxious Children." *Journal of Cognitive Psychotherapy: An International Quarterly.* 19: 379–392.

Semple, R. J., J. Lee, D. Rosa, and L. Miller. 2010. "A Randomized Trial of Mindfulness-Based Cognitive Therapy for Children: Promoting Mindful Attention to Enhance Social-Emotional Resiliency in Children." *Journal of Child and Family Studies* 19: 218–229.

Shapiro, L. 2004. *101 Ways to Teach Children Social Skills: A Ready-to-Use, Reproducible Activity Book*. The Bureau for At-Risk Youth. USA. Retrieved March 3, 2015 from: http://www.socialskillscentral.com/free/101_Ways_Teach_Children_Social_Skills.pdf

Siegel, D. 2007. *The Mindful Brain: Reflection and Attunement in the Cultivation of Well-Being*. New York: W. W. Norton and Company.

Smith, B., B. S. G. Molina, and W. Pelham. 2002. "The Clinically Meaningful Link Between Alcohol Use and Attention Deficit Hyperactivity Disorder." *Alcohol Research and Health* 26:2, National Institutes of Health. Retrieved 01/10/16 from http://pubs.niaaa.nih.gov/publications/arh26–2/122–129.pdf

Stahl, B, and E. Goldstein. 2010. *A Mindfulness-Based Stress Reduction Workbook*. Oakland, CA: New Harbinger Publications, Inc.

Thompson, M. and J. Gauntlett-Gilbert. 2008. "Mindfulness with Children and Adolescents: Effective Clinical Application." *Clinical Child Psychology and Psychiatry* 13: 395–407.

US Department of Education. "Teaching Children with Attention Deficit Hyperactivity Disorder: Instructional Strategies and Practices. How to Implement the Strategy: Behavioral Interventions." Retrieved Feb. 25, 2015 from: http://www2.ed.gov/rschstat/research/pubs/adhd/adhd-teaching.html

Van der Oord, S., S. Bögels, and D. Peijnenburg. 2012. "The Effectiveness of Mindfulness Training for Children with ADHD and Mindful Parenting for Their Parents." *Journal of Child and Family Studies* 21: 139–147. Retrieved 9/5/13 http://www.ncbi.nlm.nih.gov/pmc/articles/PMC3267931/

Wagner, E. E., J. H. Rathus, and A. L. Miller. 2006. "Mindfulness in Dialectical Behavior Therapy (DBT) for Adolescents." In *Mindfulness-Based Treatment Approaches: Clinician's Guide to Evidence Base and Applications*, edited by R. A. Baer. Oxford, UK: Elsevier.

Wall, R. B. 2005. "Tai Chi and Mindfulness-Based Stress Reduction in a Boston Public Middle School." *Journal of Pediatric Health Care* 19: 230–237.

Weiss, M., and J. Salpekar. 2010. "Sleep Problems in the Child with Attention-Deficit Hyperactivity Disorder: Defining Aetiology and Appropriate Treatments." *CNS Drugs* 24: 811–828.

Wheeler, J., and C. L. Carlson. 1994. "The Social Functioning of Children With ADD With Hyperactivity and ADD Without Hyperactivity: A Comparison of Their Peer Relations and Social Deficits." *Journal of Emotional and Behavioral Disorders* 2: 2–12.

Zylowska, L., D. Ackerman, M. Yang, J. Futrell, N. Horton, T. Hale, C. Pataki, and S. Smalley. 2008. "Mindfulness Meditation Training in Adults and Adolescents with ADHD: A Feasibility Study." *Journal of Attention Disorders* 11: 737–746.

Debra Burdick, LCSW, also known as "The Brain Lady," is an international expert on mindfulness and attention deficit/hyperactivity disorder (ADHD). She is author of *ADHD Non-Medication Treatment and Skills for Children and Teens*; *Mindfulness Skills for Kids and Teens*; *Mindfulness Skills Workbook for Clinicians and Clients*; and several mindfulness CDs. She teaches all-day workshops, including *100 Brain-Changing Mindfulness Strategies for Clinical Practice*, *Childhood ADHD: Advanced Non-Drug Treatments and Strategies that Change the Brain*, and *Mindfulness Toolkit for Kids and Teens*.

A licensed clinical social worker and board-certified neurotherapist, Debra recently retired from private practice to focus on writing and speaking. She incorporates mindfulness skills in all areas of her life and work, and has extensive experience helping children and adults with ADHD, including her own daughter.

An expert author on www.selfgrowth.com, Debra's work has been featured on radio (Attention Talk Radio, ADHD Support Talk Radio, and Doctors of the USA), in print media (*The Wall Street Journal*, Connecticut newspaper *The Day*, and *Self-Improvement*), and on TV (*Parenting Powers* and *Restoring Health Holistically*).

Visit www.thebrainlady.com for more information.

Foreword writer **Lara Honos-Webb, PhD**, is a worldwide attention deficit disorder (ADD) expert, and offers ADD coaching. She is a clinical psychologist and author of *The Gift of ADHD*, *The Gift of ADHD Activity Book*, *The Gift of Adult ADD*, *The ADHD Workbook for Teens*, and *Listening to Depression*. She has published more than twenty-five scholarly articles. Learn more about her work at www.addisagift.com.

Register your **new harbinger** titles for additional benefits!

When you register your **new harbinger** title—purchased in any format, from any source—you get access to benefits like the following:

- Downloadable accessories like printable worksheets and extra content

- Instructional videos and audio files

- Information about updates, corrections, and new editions

Not every title has accessories, but we're adding new material all the time.

Access free accessories in 3 easy steps:

1. Sign in at NewHarbinger.com (or **register** to create an account).

2. Click on **register a book**. Search for your title and click the **register** button when it appears.

3. Click on the **book cover or title** to go to its details page. Click on **accessories** to view and access files.

That's all there is to it!

If you need help, visit:

NewHarbinger.com/accessories

new harbinger
CELEBRATING
40 YEARS